THE MYSTICAL *I*

OTHER WRITINGS OF JOEL S. GOLDSMITH

The Art of Meditation

The Art of Spiritual Healing

Gift of Love

The Infinite Way

Living the Infinite Way

Our Spiritual Resources

Practicing the Presence

The Thunder of Silence

The World Is New

THE MYSTICAL *I*

Joel S. Goldsmith

EDITED BY LORRAINE SINKLER

HarperSanFrancisco
A Division of HarperCollins*Publishers*

 For information address HarperCollins Publishers, 10 East 53rd Street, New York, NY 10022.

FIRST HARPERCOLLINS PAPERBACK EDITION PUBLISHED IN 1993

Library of Congress Cataloging-in-Publication Data

Goldsmith, Joel S.
The mystical I / Joel S. Goldsmith. — 1st HarperCollins pbk. ed.
p. cm.
Originally published: 1st ed. New York : Harper & Row, 1971.
ISBN 0–06–250818–0 (pbk. : alk. paper)
1. New Thought. I. Title.
BF639.G5683 1993
248.2'2—dc20 92–56124

---

93 94 95 96 97 RRD(H) 10 9 8 7 6 5 4 3 2 1

This edition is printed on acid-free paper that meets the American National Standards Institute Z39.48 Standard.

Except the Lord build the house,
they labour in vain that build it.
—Psalm 127

Illumination dissolves all material ties and binds men together with the golden chains of spiritual understanding; it acknowledges only the leadership of the Christ; it has no ritual or rule but the divine, impersonal universal Love, no other worship than the inner Flame that is ever lit at the shrine of Spirit. This union is the free state of spiritual brotherhood. The only restraint is the discipline of Soul; therefore, we know liberty without license; we are a united universe without physical limits, a divine service to God without ceremony or creed. The illumined walk without fear—by Grace.

—*The Infinite Way*

CONTENTS

THE MYSTICAL *I*

Behold, I stand at the door, and knock: if any man hear my voice, and open the door, I will come in to him, and I will sup with him, and he with me.

—*Revelations 3:20*

CHAPTER I

I STAND AT THE DOOR

"I stand at the door, and knock." Who is this *I* standing at the door?* And at what door is this *I* standing? At what door but the door of your consciousness? *I* stand at the door of your consciousness and knock, but you must open the door and admit *Me,* for "I am the bread of life. . . . I am the way, the truth, and the life. . . . I am the resurrection, and the life. . . . I am come that you might have life, and that you might have it more abundantly."

The *I* that is standing at the door of your consciousness and knocking is the *I* that has come that you might have the life more abundant. When you admit that *I* into your consciousness, you have admitted life eternal, the bread of life, the water of life, and the wine of life. You have admitted into your consciousness the power of

The material in this volume first appeared in the form of letters sent to students of The Infinite Way throughout the world as an aid to the revelation and unfoldment of the transcendental Consciousness through a deeper understanding of Scripture and the principles of The Infinite Way.—ED.

*The word *I,* italicized, refers to God, as does the word *Me,* capitalized below.

resurrection: the resurrection of your body, your home, your marriage, your fortune, and your business. Only when you admit *I* into your consciousness, do you admit into yourself the secret of life. When you acknowledge that that *I* in the midst of you is mighty, you are not speaking of a man or of any person: you are speaking of the *I, I.*

Close your eyes and within yourself, silently, sacredly, secretly, and gently say the word, *"I, I."* That *I* in the midst of you is mighty. That *I* in the midst of you is greater than any problem in the outside world. That *I* in the midst of you is come that you might have life and might have it more abundantly. That *I* has been with you since "before Abraham was," awaiting your recognition and your acknowledgment.

"Know ye not that ye are the temple of God?" Know ye not that the name of God is *I,* or *I AM,* and that you are the temple of God only when you have admitted *I* into your consciousness and held It there secretly, sacredly, gently, peaceably, so that at any moment you can close your eyes and just remember *I?**

This I *that is in the midst of me is life eternal. This* I *that is within me is the He that is mighty.*†

When Jesus speaks of the Father within and when Paul speaks of the Christ that dwells in him, they are speaking of the *I AM,* the very *I* that you are, the *I* that you have just announced, that is in the midst of you.

*In the spiritual literature of the world, the varying concepts of God are indicated by the use of such words as "Father," "Mother," "Soul," "Spirit," "Principle," "Love," and "Life." The author, therefore, has used the pronouns "He" and "It," or "Himself" and "Itself," interchangeably in referring to God.

†The italicized elements in this book are spontaneous meditations which have come to the author during periods of uplifted consciousness and are not in any sense intended to be used as affirmations, denials, or formulas. They have been inserted here from time to time to serve as examples of the free flowing of the Spirit. As the reader practices the Presence, he too, in his exalted moments, will receive ever new and fresh inspiration as the outpouring of the Spirit.

The Personal Sense of "I" and the Divine I

The way to avoid suffering from a dose of egotism and to differentiate between the egotistical "I"—the "I" that believes it has power, that it has sufficient wisdom to run the world or even sufficient wisdom to run its own life—and this *I* in the midst of every one of us, this gentle *I* that you are voicing, is to remember that you cannot use or influence God, but by your yielding to that divine *I,* God can use you.

God can influence, guide, direct, feed, clothe, and house you. Your heavenly Father, the *I* that you are, knows that you have need of these things, and it is His good pleasure to give you the Kingdom. Therefore, if the ego strikes at you so that even for a moment you believe God is subject to your will, remember quickly that it is not your will that is to be done, but God's will, and God's will can be done only in the degree of your yielding to this *I* that is within you.

The Resurrecting Power of I

When you hold the word *I* in your consciousness, no evil can come nigh your dwelling place, and even though you are crucified, you will be resurrected. If the temple of your body is destroyed, in three days *I* will build it up again. *I* will build it—not the personal sense of "I," but *I* will build it up again. Your little "I" must be still so that *I* in the midst of you can perform Its mighty works.

If your business is lost, if your house or your family is lost, in three days—probably not literally three days, but in a short length of time —*I* in the midst of you will raise it up if only you can be still, not resist the evil, not fight the danger that threatens you, and let that *I* that you are, that *I* that is your true identity, take over. Whether the problem comes in the form of sin or disease, lack or drought, depression or business recession, it has only the "arm of flesh."

Sometimes the mesmerism of the world is so strong that almost any person may come under its influence, but as long as he maintains his oneness with the Source of Life which is *I AM,* even though temporarily his "temple" be wrecked, in three days it will be raised up again.

Releasing the Spiritual Glory

The message of The Infinite Way is wholly dedicated to admitting the presence of the Christ into consciousness, and letting It transform us from the human sense of life to the spiritual, not merely changing a bad human sense of life to a good human sense of life. Our interest is not in that direction. Our interest is in surrendering the whole of material sense, even when it is good, and receiving in exchange our divine sonship. The goal of The Infinite Way is to become the son of God, not merely a healthy human being, a good human being, or a wealthy human being, but rather to show in our daily experience our spiritual nature, that which actually was given to us in the beginning: "the glory which I had with thee before the world was," the spiritual glory. That is what we are praying for.

"I stand at the door, and knock" means that the presence and power of God, the Christ, stands at the door of your consciousness seeking admittance. Your function is to answer, "Enter, Lord. 'Speak, Lord; for thy servant heareth.' I am opening the door of my consciousness that the Christ, the son of God, may enter, that the Spirit may be upon me, and that I may be redeemed. Thy grace is my sufficiency; therefore I am not here seeking health, wealth, harmony, or peace. It is only Thy grace and Thy will that I seek, that Thy Spirit may be upon me, within me, shining through me, and then let It take whatever form It will."

In your human experience, the presence of God may seem to have done nothing for you, but now open your consciousness specifically that the Spirit of God may enter and perform Its will within you. This opening of consciousness is prayer, or contemplative meditation.

You are contemplating truth, acknowledging the presence and power of God, acknowledging that the Lord is standing at the door awaiting your invitation to enter and to transform your life, not as you would have it transformed, but as it will be transformed when the Spirit of God makes you over into Its image and likeness.

Restoring the Lost Years

"He performeth the thing that is appointed for me." The promise does not say that God will do what you would like to have done: the promise is that God will perform that which He has appointed for you. Since you cannot read the mind of God, you must turn within in this realization: " 'Not my will, but thine, be done.' Whatever it is that I am ordained to do, whatever it is Thou hast for me, Thou performest for me, within me, through me." Then take a period for listening so that the Spirit may be upon you and continue to perform Its work through you.

It is true that, just as you can with physical force accomplish a great deal that you would like to do, so you can with mental force also accomplish much that you would like to do; but if you wish to be under the law of God and the grace of God, it is necessary that you accept God as the divine Intelligence of this universe, and not seek to inform, tell, or advise It. Rather be still, and know that *I* at the center of your being am God, and then rest in confidence that His will is being done in you.

Be still! Do not pray with words; do not pray with thoughts; be still! Let the Christ enter and purify, redeem, wipe clean, and restore "the years that the locust hath eaten." Let the Christ do it: do not try to help, inform, or instruct It. Be still!

It will gently remind you: "*I* stood at the door and knocked, but now the door is opened, and *I* am within. *I* am 'closer . . . [to you] than breathing, and nearer than hands and feet.' "* That *I* is the very

*Alfred Tennyson.

presence and power of God, the very Spirit of God, and It, the All-knowing, is within. Do you know why It is there? Do you know why this Christ, the Spirit of God, is come to you?

The Master gave the reason: "I am come that they might have life, and that they might have it more abundantly." *I,* the presence of God, *I,* who am standing at the door and knocking, *I*, whom you have admitted into your consciousness, *I* am come within you that you might have life and have it more abundantly. Your function is to rest and relax in this truth that the presence of God within you is there for that one purpose.

It makes no difference what your past life has been, or what your present life is, up to the moment of admitting the Christ. Do not be concerned or worried about your past mistakes, errors, or sins; they are not being counted against you. For each person, as the Christ enters, the past no longer exists: past sins are forgiven and wiped out, along with the penalty for them, and a new day begins. "Though your sins be as scarlet, they shall be as white as snow." Therefore do not burden yourself with guilt complexes. Make whatever form of restitution or expression of regret is possible for any past offense, but then drop it. Drop it!

You cannot live yesterday again; you cannot live even an hour ago, and all you do is torture yourself by bringing the memory of yesterday into today. If you do not bring it there, it can never get there, because yesterday is gone, and it can be revived only in memory. No one can do that but you, and no one can drop it but you. In the moment that you admit the Christ, yesterday is gone, and the capacity for sin, for error, or for committing offenses of any kind has also gone. In His presence is fulfillment; in His presence is peace; in His presence is harmony. There cannot be the presence of God in you and the capacity for error. That cannot be! You either exclude *Me,* the Spirit of God, the Christ of God, or you admit *Me:* "I stand at the door, and knock."

"Choose you this day whom ye will serve!" Open your consciousness—"Speak, Lord; for thy servant heareth." Let this be repeated ten, twenty, or thirty times a day, until the Christ has so filled you and so fills every nook and cranny of your consciousness that there is no room even for a remembrance of yesterday. Then the Christ which you have admitted restores to you whatever it is that you have lost of peace, harmony, health, abundance, happiness, or companionship. All is restored, and in a more fulfilling way than before, because heretofore you had these things only materially. Now you will have them spiritually, and that means without limit and without harm or destruction to another.

When you are fulfilled through the presence and power of God and God's grace, it is not at anyone else's expense nor at the cost of his loss or destruction; rather, what benefits you benefits all who come within range of your consciousness. We do not take *from* one another; we share, and what we share is that presence of the Christ within us: "Son . . . all that I have is thine."

And now the Christ within says, "My peace I give unto you." That Voice within speaks to you and says, "*My* peace"—that is, spiritual peace—"I give unto you"—not the peace that the world gives. If you are looking for the peace of the world, do not go to the Christ for it, because the peace that *I,* the Christ, give you is a peace that the world cannot give. The world might flood you with money, honors, or fame; but it will leave you hollow inside, unsatisfied, incomplete. But when you feel *My* peace,* you will feel it abundantly, permanently, joyously, a peace that passes human understanding. Then you will understand why "My grace is sufficient for thee." There is no lack where God's grace is.

"My peace I give unto you" is spoken from within you to you, from the center of your being out to the circumference: *My* wholeness I give unto thee; *My* immortality I give unto thee; *My* infinity I give unto thee. Never do *I* withhold: all this is thine. Allness is the measure of God's gifts to individual you and me as we open ourselves to receive them.

*The word "My," capitalized, refers to God.

Givingness As a Measure of Receptivity

When the grace of God is upon you, can you not realize that you are a light unto all those who are in darkness? You are safety to those who are in danger; you are healing and health to those who are sick; you are prosperity to those who are poor, not by virtue of yourself—of yourself you are nothing—but by the grace of God which is within, by the Spirit of God that is upon you. You are ordained to heal the sick, to raise the dead, to help the poor by the Spirit of God to which you have opened yourself. Then all those who reach out to your consciousness receive that same spiritual blessing in proportion to their receptivity.

But how can they become more receptive to God, to the Christ, to this spiritual Influence? How can you become more receptive? By increasing your givingness. Receptivity is attained only through giving, through pouring out from the center of your being, and the more you give, the more receptive you are to the grace, the presence, and the healing power of God. What you have to give is an individual matter. The question that comes to you then is, "How am I to give? Out of what? I have so little."

And the answer is, "That is not true. You have much to give. You have the grace of God; you have all of God, for God has given you all of Himself."

The Master has told us some of the things that can be given: forgiveness, prayer. Learn to give forgiveness over and over and over again to your friends and to your enemies. You can pray; you can pray for your enemies. This is another form of giving: praying that your enemies be released from penalties, praying that their consciousness be opened to the light, praying that their sins be forgiven them, even as you would have your sins forgiven you.

Receptivity is the key to spiritual attainment, and receptivity is attained through givingness. If you have a little change or more than a little to give, give and share it where you will. Remember, however, that givingness is not only the giving of material things, but is your attitude of forgiving, benevolence, peace, and good will toward all men. This is the real givingness: good will toward men, setting all men free, and holding no one in condemnation. It does not mean that you are not aware of the sins that are going on around you; it means that you stop holding man in condemnation to them.

In opening consciousness, a Presence comes in. You may not at first be aware of It as an actual Presence, but eventually you will, because It is a Presence, It is a Spirit. You do not see It, hear It, taste It, touch It, or smell It, but you experience It, and as It floods you It brings healing of mind and body. It brings purification to a decadent moral sense; It brings with It a greater integrity; It washes you clean of the negative thoughts and feelings which none of us enjoy having, but which even the best of us have.

Secrecy Imperative

Those who learn that *I* at the center of their being stand at the door of consciousness and knock, those who open their consciousness and let this *I* in, must then close their mouths so that It does not escape. Always keep that *I* sacred and secret within yourself and watch your life become transformed. Then, as you find those who you yourself discover are truly seeking this way of life, do not hesitate to share with them the secret. To others give a cup of cold water, but be sure that you are not offering them the "pearl" of great price, which this is, because by prematurely letting this secret out of your own consciousness you can sometimes lose it. It is possible to lose it for yourself and never regain it again in this experience.

When I impart this work to you, I am merely planting in your consciousness the seed of truth. It is you who must hold this seed of truth deep in your consciousness. Nurture it by consciously remembering it; nurture it by consciously declaring it within yourself; nurture it by keeping it sacred and secret within you, never forgetting under any circumstances to let your last word at night be, "Thank You, Father, for the *I* that dwelleth in me."

Repentance, the Way of Return

It is never the *I,* the *I AM,* God, that deserts you; it is never This that abandons you. There is no sin that you could commit deep or scarlet enough that would compel God, the *I AM*, to forsake you. The sins you commit compel you to forsake God because you cannot face Him with the sins. Once you know this, you will face Him again with repentance because Scripture reveals that the way of return to your conscious oneness with God is through repentance.

Look to the Master within you and say, "Forgive me." Acknowledge the wrong, whether in spoken words or just through the eyes. Let the Master know that you are ready to be taken back to heaven, and then you will find that you are again one with the Father. Though your sins have been scarlet, they will be white as snow the moment you close your eyes and look within to the *I:* "Father, forgive me, I knew not what I was doing." Like the Prodigal Son, you will find that as you reach out one per cent of the way toward your Father's house, your Father will come out the other 99 per cent of the way to meet you, to robe you and ring you once again with the royal robe and the royal ring.

Everyone has sinned. No one is without sin. Even those who consider themselves the most righteous have sinned even though they may be ignorant of how they sinned. But they have; we have; and perhaps even now we are sinning. This can make no separation between us and our Father, however, because if we have sinned seventy times seven we can still look up and say, "Father, forgive me. I knew not what I was doing." And as long as we turn to the Father, to that *I,* we are once more at one with our Source, because *I AM* is our Father.

If there should be any temptation to sin, to be sick, or to die, any temptation to yield to any discord on earth, any temptation to falter if you are called upon to face thieves, burglars, or murderers, and if at that moment you hold this *I* sacredly within you, I can assure you no harm will come nigh your dwelling place because you are dwelling in "the secret place of the most High."

If you will live in the consciousness of this *I* abiding in you, you will find that you and your Father are consciously one. This means that you are one with infinite individual power; you are one with infinite individual wisdom; you are one with infinite guidance. You are one with all that God is as long as you are dwelling in that "secret place," keeping this great truth so sacred within that no one can tell that you know it, except that by the look on your face he will know you have discovered the mystery of life and found peace everlasting.

My *Peace*

Men have tried to achieve peace: peace of mind, peace of soul, peace of body. They have tried to find security and safety in every material way there is under the sun, and yet the world today has less of peace than ever in its history. The world has less of safety and security than at any time ever before, and there is only one reason. The world is further away today than it has ever been from acknowledging that it is *I* who have been standing at the door and knocking.

If you admit Me *and abide in me* Me *and let* Me *abide in you, then* I *am your safety, your security, your peace, your meat, wine, and water.*

"My peace I give unto you: not as the world giveth, give I unto you." Where does this "My peace" come from except from Me, *and how would it come from* Me *if* I *were not in you?* I *in thee, and thou in* Me. *As you abide in this conscious realization that* I *abide in you, you abide in* Me, *and we are one. Then all that* I, *God, am becomes your experience. All that* I *have becomes yours. All* My *peace becomes your peace.*

"My kingdom is not of this world." "My kingdom," the kingdom of the I *that* I AM, My *kingdom, the Christ kingdom, the spiritual kingdom, is not of this world. "My thoughts are not your thoughts, neither are your ways*

my ways." My *peace* I *give unto you because* I *am within you, and you are within* Me, *for we are one.*

All this is that *I* speaking to you, the very *I* that has been knocking at the door of your consciousness, seeking admittance since "before Abraham was." When you have admitted that *I* into your consciousness, then all the *I* is, you are. All the *I* has is yours.

For this reason, as we meet together for a spiritual purpose, we can share with one another. Whatever of divine Grace touches one consciousness is immediately a part of the consciousness of everyone who is receptive. We are gathered in one place, in one mind, in one spirit, all of one household. As the Holy Ghost descends upon one of us, it touches the receptive thought of everyone who is present, for we are one family.

That which unites us and makes of us one family is our admitting into our consciousness the *I* that has stood at the door and knocked.

Open the Door of the Consciousness of the World

All the evil of the world has come about because of a sense of separation from God. We have accepted man on earth and God in heaven, and thereby have separated ourselves in belief from God, instead of being able to walk up and down this world knowing:

> *I and the Father are so one that if I stand before Pilate, I can say, "Thou couldest have no power at all against me, except it were given thee from above."*

Before Pilate, the greatest temporal power of the universe? Yes, even he could have no power over us unless it were given him of God. Daniel could walk into the lion's den, and the lions could do nothing to him because he held aloft the *I* and knew that *I* in the midst of him was mighty.

You, too, can face any situation that arises in your life—anything from a family situation to a national or international situation—if you can learn to sit quietly and lift up the *I*. Lift up the *I*, and realize that as long as you are abiding in that *I*, as long as you are abiding in that Presence, no evil can come nigh your world.

In My *presence is fulfillment. In* My *presence is fullness of light, and as long as you have that Presence lifted up in you, evil not only cannot come nigh your dwelling place, it cannot come nigh your entire world.*

We do not have to wait for three billion people to learn this truth in order to save the world. A little handful of us can uphold this *I*, can live with this *I* within us, and face the world with It. Watch the evils of this world dissolve, the evils in personal enemies, national and international enemies. But to witness this, somebody must hold up the banner of *I;* somebody must admit the *I* that is knocking at the door of the consciousness of this whole world seeking entrance.

Now let us go beyond each one of us individually and let us remember that this *I* that is knocking at the door of the entire world at this minute and begging to be admitted is God. What we must do —a little group of us—is to open this world to the presence of *I*. Open the door and say, "Father, come in, for in Thy presence there is no warfare. In Thy presence is peace. In Thy presence is fulfillment." Open the door of your consciousness. Open the door of this universe and admit God, for this world is suffering from only one thing: the absence of God.

All the while It, the presence of God, is saying to us, *"I* am standing at the door begging, begging to be admitted." All we have to do is open our consciousness and say, "Father, enter. Enter this world; enter human consciousness." Let us acknowledge that there is an *I* knocking at the door of this world. Let us open the door and admit God, and you will soon see how rapidly the sins, the diseases, the lacks, and the limitations of this world will disappear.

In My *presence is fulfillment.* My *peace I give unto you, but how can* I *give it to you, if you do not admit* Me *into your consciousness? How can* I *give it to you?*

Open the door of your consciousness; open the door of the consciousness of this world and let the Father in. Then watch this silent, sacred, secret Influence as It permeates all human consciousness and eventually reveals peace. Peace will not come through man. Peace will not come through treaties. Peace will not come through armaments. Peace will not come through disarmament. Peace will come only through opening the door of consciousness and letting *Me,* the Father, in.

CHAPTER II

THE UNVEILING

Moses was given a revelation of absolute truth. It was, in fact, a revelation of the final and ultimate truth, and the proof of this is that through this truth he was able to take the Hebrews out of slavery and lead them right up to the Promised Land, not by means of armies or with storehouses of food, but entirely under the grace of God. This is one of the most remarkable demonstrations of Grace in all religious history. It was a mass freeing of people, completed under the grace of God, without force of arms and without even an organized activity. Only the unveiling of ultimate truth could yield such fruitage.

But after that great experience the truth was again veiled, so that not until centuries later did the Master Christ Jesus remove the veil and again reveal the truth. This truth enabled him to heal, to supply, and also to pass on to his disciples and apostles the ability to heal and to give freedom, so that for three hundred years after Jesus' ministry on earth, the unveiled truth was known, and more and more people came into their freedom because they knew the truth.

About 300 A.D., however, the truth was veiled again, and it has been kept so well veiled that no religion known to man has revealed that truth in the past nearly seventeen hundred years. True, in part, here and there in modern times, it has been known, but on the whole the truth has remained veiled.

Truth can be known only by its fruitage. Only in that way can you know whether or not a teaching or a religion is truth. If it sets its followers free physically, mentally, morally, and financially, if it brings greater freedom and harmony in their human relationships, if it makes them less subject to the rule of man, to the sway of nature, or to the laws of matter and mind, then you can know that they are getting closer and closer to truth.

"By their fruits ye shall know them." The Master made it very clear that under certain conditions man would bear fruit richly. Under other conditions, he would be as a branch of a tree that is cut off, withers, and dies. You yourself must be the judge as to whether the people of this world have been bearing fruit richly in the past seventeen hundred years or whether generation after generation has been like the branch that withers and dies.

Spirit Cannot Be Personalized

What is truth? What is the veil placed upon truth that acts to hold us in bondage to ignorance and to fear? What is truth? If you study the religions of the world and if you go back carefully to the original revelators of each teaching, you will discover that there is only one truth, and that each one of these revelators received and taught the same truth. Whether it is the teaching of Krishna, of Buddha, of Shankara, of Moses, or of Jesus, you will discover that it was always the same truth. It has never deviated. Then, if you go further in your study of why and how these revelations were veiled and what manner of veil was put on them, you will discover that it was the same veil, that the same method was used in each case to hide the truth.

Every time truth has been revealed, those to whom it was revealed have identified the truth with the name of the revelator and worshiped him. The revelator never did this, because anyone who is high enough in consciousness to receive such a revelation would never personalize it. In fact, no person could be an open channel to receive such a revelation if he were even tempted to use it for personal gain or aggrandizement. But there are others possibly who, either through ignorance or evil intent, decide to build a statue to Moses, Elijah, Jesus, or some other revelator, and then the veil is on again.

Jesus removed the veil, and he did it so that the truth would be perfectly clear throughout all ages. On the one hand he said, "I can of mine own self do nothing. . . . If I bear witness of myself, my witness is not true. . . . My doctrine is not mine, but his that sent me." All this he said so that for all time men might see, and seeing, understand that his *human* identity was the same as yours and mine. But he also said, "I am the way, the truth, and the life. . . . He that seeth me seeth him that sent me. . . . I am come that they might have life, and that they might have it more abundantly. . . . I am the resurrection, and the life. . . ."

To the unillumined, those two sets of statements seem irreconcilable, but there is a way to interpret them so that they are no longer contradictory. For example, if I say that I am a man of flesh and blood as you are, that I have my human failings and my human virtues even as you have, that is undoubtedly true of the man Joel. And yet, at the same time, the *I*, the spiritual identity of that man Joel, is God—just as the *I* of every man is God. Because of that, you may receive healings through a person who knows that truth. You may be reformed; you may overcome false appetites; you may have your business made better; you may have your family life made happier because *I* in the midst of him is God. If you turn to the Christ, the *I* at the center of any illumined person will give you water, and you will never thirst again. *I* will give you food, meat, water, bread, and you will never hunger again.

One Father

The final revelation that must forever remove the veil and show you the real truth is the Master's statement, "Call no man your father upon the earth." This sets aside the claim that he was the only child of God and that he alone was divine, and reveals to you that your real Source, your real Creator, is the same as that of Jesus or of Gautama the Buddha, who was also claimed to have been immaculately conceived. Therefore, if you can accept the revelation of Jesus Christ that Spirit alone is your father, your creator, then we are brothers and sisters of Christ and in Christ; we are members of one household, one family with God the Father, and we the children. We are heirs and joint-heirs.

Therefore hearken to this: "I and my Father are one." But the Master has also said, "Call no man your father upon the earth." Now what must you say? You and your Father must also be one. So, whether you are Jew or Gentile, Oriental or Occidental, white or black, poor or rich, high or low, if you accept the truth of the message "I and my Father are one," that means that your relationship to God is oneness, regardless of what your immediate demonstration of that truth may be.

I, *Individualized*

When you are given the courage to recognize your true identity, you will begin to understand the nature of this message which is all bound up in one word: *I.* You will withdraw your gaze from "man, whose breath is in his nostrils," and you will learn to awaken in the morning gleefully with a song of praise in your heart.

Thank You, Father, for another day to prove that I and Thou art one, for another day to show forth Thy kingdom, Thy riches, Thy harmony, Thy health—not mine. Of my own self, I have no health; of my own self, I have no wealth; of my own self, I have no virtue. There is but one good, and that is the I *of my own being.*

When I unveil the truth of the *I* of your being as God, the son of God, and Christ as the mediator, the individualization, the connecting link between *I,* the Father, and *I,* the son, I am revealing the truth that sets you free. Should some students in the future claim that Joel is their master, you will recognize what they are doing. They are putting the veil back on the truth: somebody either wants to get rich or powerful, or somebody is very stupid. It has to be either an evil purpose or it has to be stupidity.

Some have put the veil back on the truth through stupidity, through ignorance of the meaning of the word *I,* and through personalizing It. Others have put the veil on ignorantly by trying to worship somebody and thinking that was humility. But what is true humility? Humility is recognizing that a spiritual teacher is the Christ of God. That is humility because it leads to the next truth, "And so am I." But to say that only one man is the Christ of God is not humility; it is stupidity.

Such a teaching as this cannot be taught. You cannot get up on a platform and tell this to the crowds assembled, nor can you go into the churches or the universities and teach it there, because the three-dimensional mind cannot receive it. Neither can you go out and proselyte. The only way in which this can be taught is as I have taught it. First, came the revelation of it, which I kept locked up secretly and sacredly within me until such time as I was showing it forth in my life. Then, without any advertising or any seeking, students began coming to me. How they found me is a mystery of God, but they did, and they came and said, "You have something. Share it with me."

Then, I fed it to them a little at a time, showing by precept, example, and demonstration that it was true, and finally after ten or eleven years so much of it was absorbed that I could completely remove the veil by saying, "He that hath seen me hath seen the

Father." Those who heard did not go away and misinterpret the message, because throughout all the years they have seen that I have not been setting myself apart from them, but have been revealing that every truth spoken about Jesus Christ or any of the saints or sages of the past or present is the truth to be realized about every person.

Only One Divine Selfhood

Your responsibility, first of all, is to take the word *I* sacredly and secretly into your consciousness, if so be the rightness of this strikes you. Keep that truth locked up within you until bit by bit the lines begin to fade away from your cheeks if they are there, the worry begins to leave your forehead if it is there, the fear begins to drop away from your mind and your heart if it is there; and all of a sudden you discover that there is a Presence that has gone before you to "make the crooked places straight" without your consciously sending It there.

Then you will discover why Scripture emphasizes that God is not in the whirlwind: God is in the "still small voice." Where is the still small voice? The Master tells us that the abiding place of God is neither "Lo here!" nor "Lo there!" —not in holy mountains or in holy temples, but within you. This is where the still small voice is: within you.

It may take a month, a year, or ten years before you can break the crust of personal sense and finally hear that still small voice within yourself, but when you do, it says to you, "Be still, and know that I am God." It does not say that Joel or Mary is God. No, no! It does not say that William or Robert is God, or Mildred. It always says *I.* And do you know what else it says? "Fear not, for I am with thee. . . . I will never leave thee, nor forsake thee." Fear not. Though your sins be scarlet, in the moment of your recognition of *I* in the midst of you, you are white as snow.

If you are the best human being on the face of the earth, you are no closer to heaven than the worst one. No human being will get into the kingdom of God, even if he is as good as John the Baptist. The least of those who recognize their oneness with the Father is greater than John the Baptist, even though he was the greatest Hebrew prophet. Why? Because he still had a God separate and apart from himself. He still looked upon someone else as the light of the world instead of saying, "Ah, yes, indeed! He is the light because he has recognized the light and is revealing to us: 'Go, and do thou likewise.' "

The unveiled truth in every age has always been the revelation that *I* am He: there is no other. There is only one Ego, only one Selfhood, the *I AM THAT I AM,* that *I* in the midst of us, the divine Selfhood of you and of me. The veil has always descended when that title has been draped on some one person and all the others have been looked upon as worms in the dust, whereas the truth is that *I* is God Itself.

It would make no difference if you were to refer to *I* as the son of God, because God the Father and God the son are one. In the beginning it may help us if we realize, "I am the son of God, heir of God, joint-heir to all the heavenly riches." Probably it was only in the very last stages of his spiritual development and because of his realized oneness that the Master could say, "He that hath seen me hath seen the Father."

To be sure that no one misses the way, we caution our students never to say, even to themselves, "I am God." It is not even wise to voice such a statement as "I am the son of God." The ideal way is just to say, *"I,"* and think of what It means. Then in time, as the listening ear is developed, you will hear the Voice say, "*I* in the midst of you am God. *I* who am closer to you than breathing am God." When you hear this, you have made contact with your Source. Usually, if you merely repeat the words, you are just saying them out of the mind or the intellect, and when they come out of that mind or intellect they are not true. It is only as they come forth from the Spirit of God Itself in you that they are truth.

Secretly Abide in the Truth of Your I*-ness*

This is the age in which truth is revealing itself in us, to us, and through us. This is the age. This message is not mine; I did not invent it, discover it, or create it. It was a revelation, and it is carrying itself around the world. Furthermore, this truth which is now being revealed in consciousness is being revealed not merely in my consciousness but also in yours, and not through my consciousness alone but also through yours. You need not speak it; you need not voice it; you need not proselyte with it. You need only abide with it. Abide with this Word within you, and you will be preaching it in the silence to all who are receptive. You, in your lifetime, may never know who receives it.

My experience has been that when this truth is revealed in my consciousness and held there sacredly, somebody feels it somewhere. In some way or other, those who are receptive and responsive to the truth will be led to it, whether to a person or to a book.

The responsibility that is on your shoulders is not to go out into the world to teach or preach it because that is not for you to decide but for God. Your responsibility lies in so living it that you demonstrate it, and that is all. From there on, the *I* which is your divine Consciousness knows your need and will lead you into your rightful activity. It will lead you in the way in which you should go.

When Pilate asked the Master, "What is truth?" the Master remained silent. How could he say to Pilate—to any Pilate—"I am . . . the truth"? As a matter of fact, I should very much dislike to say it even to most of my students. Nevertheless, spiritual discernment does reveal that *I* is the truth, and It is the only truth there is. *I* in the midst of you is the truth: *I* in the midst of me, *I* in the midst of those in prison, *I* in the midst of those in the hospital, *I* in the midst of those in mental institutions. *I* anywhere and everywhere am He.

Impersonalize Good and Evil

By this recognition God, Good, is impersonalized and made universal; and impersonalization is one of the great principles of The Infinite Way. Impersonalize evil so that you know no man, woman, or child as evil. Evil is the activity of the belief in two powers, that which has been called the carnal or mortal mind, and because we have been born into that, it sometimes operates in you and in me to a degree, sometimes greater, sometimes lesser. But even so, there is no reason to say that I am evil or you are evil. In fact, you cannot say that I am evil when you now know that the *I* is God. To say that *I* am evil would be like saying that *I* am sick. Is that not impossible? Imagine the son of God sick, poor, dead! You can almost laugh at that because it is so ridiculous.

You may think that lack or limitation is tempting you, or sin, false appetite, or sickness, but you cannot say, "I am sick or poor or sinful." As a matter of fact, you cannot even say, "I am good or I am evil." God knows neither goodness nor badness, neither health nor sickness because *I* is incorporeal eternality.

Abide in the word *I*. Let this *I* abide in you and recognize Its identity. Never let anyone veil It for you again. Keep It sacred and secret. That is why, when I was given this mission, the final words given me at my initiation were these: "Never seek a student. Share freely with those who come to you." That has been the basis of The Infinite Way from its beginning: it has not been advertised; it has not sought to go out into the world to correct it, reform it, or change it. It has waited patiently through the years for those ready to receive Grace to come and receive It.

Seek only to demonstrate God, and the things—health, supply, companionship, home, and happiness—will be added unto you.

I *in the midst of me is God, and I can rest and relax in the assurance that* I *in the midst of me will never leave me, nor forsake me. "If I ascend up into heaven,"* I *will be there; and "if I make my bed in hell,"* I *will be there. If "I walk through the valley of the shadow of death,"* I *will be there.*

When you can rest and relax in that, you can go forward because it is not a matter of whether or not you remain on earth forever. Neither life nor death can separate you from the love of God; neither life nor death can separate you from the *I* of your being. Therefore, in what the world calls death or the next experience, whatever it may be, you will still be about your Father's business to the extent of your realization of *I.*

The Universality of I

Over and over again in the Writings, you have read that I have never in my entire lifetime given a treatment to anyone, and I have not. Why? Now you must know my secret: the *I* of me is the *I* of you. When I say that *I* will give you help, am I talking about Joel, or am I talking about the *I* of you that is within you? I am recognizing your *I*-ness. I am not saying that the *I* of me is greater than the *I* of you, and so I, Joel, will give you help. Oh no, I recognize the universal nature of *I,* and therefore if I say to you that *I* will be with you instantly, even if you are ten thousand miles away it would not make any difference. *I* will be with you because *I* am in the midst of you. *I* am closer to you than breathing.

Because of this truth, you will never have to transfer thoughts to your patients or students or to the members of your family. You have only to recognize *I* in the midst of them, and trust that *I* to perform Its function.

If you send your child or grandchild off to school and believe that the *I* of you at home is going to take care of that child out on the street, you are going to be disappointed. If you send that child out knowing that *I* in the midst of him is God and whithersoever he goes, *I* go, he will walk in his way safely.

Do you not see the meaning of what was given to us in the story of Ruth and Naomi? "Whither thou goest, I will go." No matter how you try, can you separate yourself from *I?* As you recognize *I* in me, you are recognizing my Christhood, you are praying for me, and you are treating and blessing me. As I recognize that *I* in the midst of you is your Christhood, your sonship, it is the only prayer or treatment I can utter. Otherwise, I am merely exercising the power of one mind over another, and this is no part of Infinite Way practice, which is never based on mental suggestion. It is not a practice of one mind controlling another, or of a strong mind building up a weaker mind. It is a practice in which it has been revealed to me that *I* am God. *I* in the midst of you am God. *I* in the midst of the animal world, the vegetable world, the mineral world am God, and therefore my oneness with God constitutes my oneness with all the spiritual treasures of heaven and earth. Only by virtue of my oneness with the Father do I have access to the health and wealth and abundance of all spiritual good.

The All-Sufficiency of the Grace of I

The Infinite Way teaches that you can pray for anything you like as long as it is something spiritual. This may come as a shock to you, because now you cannot pray for physical health and you cannot pray for material wealth; you cannot pray for employment; you cannot pray for happiness; and you cannot pray for a home; you can pray only for divine Grace. You are limited to praying for divine Grace. "Speak, Lord; for thy servant heareth" is a prayer. "Thy grace is my sufficiency in all things" is a prayer. To that prayer we have added: "And there is a sufficiency of Thy grace ever present in my consciousness. There is a sufficiency of Thy grace whatever prison I am in: physical, mental, moral, or financial. There is a sufficiency of Thy grace present with me now to meet the need of this moment, and sufficient unto this moment is Thy grace."

There is a reason for this. In God there is no time: there is only an eternal now. Something that is constantly now never changes. It never becomes yesterday or tomorrow. It is always now, and now there is a sufficiency of God's grace to meet the need of this moment. Your realization of that makes this a continuing moment of Grace for the next million years, because now is the only eternal time there is, and if there is a sufficiency of God's grace for this moment, and this is a continuing moment unto eternity, that is the answer. You do not have to demonstrate persons or things year after year: you have only to demonstrate God, and then you have demonstrated good unto eternity. When you have demonstrated that *I* is God, that *I* is with you forever and forever.

CHAPTER III

"I AM COME"

From the beginning of this message and from its very first book, *The Infinite Way,** it was revealed that God is not to be known but to be experienced, and only when God is experienced are there signs following or is there fruitage. You can talk about God; you can discuss God; you can even decide to change the image of God; or you can make up more synonyms for God; but all this is in the realm of toys, an intellectual game. Actually, it is a form of idolatry because it is the making of graven images, only instead of being made of gold, wood, or stone, these images are built out of the substance of thought. So one concept of God is exchanged for another concept of God, and what you end up with is not God but merely your concept of God, your thought about God.

You can see why prayer cannot be fruitful as long as it is addressed to a thought about God, an image of God, or a concept of God.

*Joel S. Goldsmith (San Gabriel, Calif.: Willing Publishing Co., Tenth Edition, 1960).

What possible difference could it make if your concept is Jewish, Vedantic, Buddhist, or Christian, as long as all you have is a concept? How can a concept answer prayer? How can a thought in your mind answer prayer?

An Image in Thought Is Not God

From the early days of modern metaphysics, "Truth" has been one of the synonyms for God, so when a person speaks of using truth it really is the same as saying, "Use God." But how can anyone *use* God? If he could, that would make him greater than God. This would also be true if the word Mind were used as a synonym for God. Do we not use the mind? If we do, does that not make us greater than mind? Consider the idea held in many quarters that thought is power. If thought is power, then thought is greater than we are, yet we are the creators of thought.

Terminology can get us into a great deal of trouble, and merely changing the terminology can get us into more trouble, for to say that that is not God, but this is, is just changing one concept or term for another. There is no use believing that one concept of God is of any greater spiritual significance than another concept of God.

In teaching that God is beyond knowing, Moses revealed a truth that must forever stand: that is, that God is incorporeal, spiritual, and therefore God cannot be known with the mind. How, then, are we to know God aright? One answer given in the Bible is that God is in the "still small voice," and this at least should give you a cue, because in the moment that you have no concept of God—nothing to pray to—when your mind is completely in a listening attitude, a vessel emptied of all its concepts, then what is revealed to you through the still small voice becomes visible to you as the harmony of spiritual living.

This, however, demands a great price. It is not only that you must permit yourself to be emptied of all concepts of God, but you also must permit yourself to be emptied of all beliefs that you know

God's plan, God's law, or God's way for you. The moment you take thought and the moment you have a desire, you set up a selfhood apart from God and thereby erect a barrier to receiving the grace of God. If you can pray, "I know not how to pray, or what things to pray for, but let Thy spirit bear intercession with my spirit," you are coming into the highest possible attitude and altitude of prayer, receptivity, and unfoldment.

"In Thy presence is fullness of joy," or fulfillment. "My grace is sufficient for thee." From these promises, do you not see that the goal of life has to be the attaining of God's presence, because only in that Presence is fulfillment? There is no way to get things separate and apart from the presence of God, not spiritual things. There is no way to live harmoniously except by Grace, and Grace is not a word; Grace is an experience. Just as God is an actual presence, so Grace is an actual experience.

Such a conviction or realization brings you to the point of transition from the metaphysical life of taking thought, of demonstrating peace, safety, security, prosperity, and happiness to the mystical consciousness of demonstrating the presence or the grace of God, which is the only legitimate demonstration on the spiritual path.

First of all, you must be willing to release God from the responsibility of doing your will. Release God from fulfilling your desires. Release God from changing or improving any phase of your humanhood, regardless of how difficult the situation may seem. Release God, and you will really not be releasing God: you will be releasing your concepts of God, which never had any possibility of fulfilling your desires.

Since you cannot know God with the mind, but you do know that the kingdom of God is within you, then wherever you are—in the prison of the body, in the prison of sin, in the prison of disease, or in the prison of poverty—right there go within and adopt this listening attitude. Then you are in a position to receive the presence and the grace of God.

As long as you have an image of God in thought or as long as you have a desire for God to fulfill, you yourself are setting up the barrier to your demonstration. It is not as if there were God *and* you. It is not as if you had to go somewhere to find God, or even be good to deserve God. All this belongs to the superstitions of the past.

I *Has No Needs*

Since I and the Father are one, I listen to the *I* that I am. That very *I* is the presence of God, and this leaves no image in thought because I have no picture of that *I.* I do not know what *I* looks like. There is no use going to a mirror, for that will not show *Me:* that will show only my body. All I can see in the mirror is my body, but *I,* who am looking at the body, am invisible, so I cannot even see my Self. I, then, only know that *I* am that Self. That Self is *I,* for we are one and not two. I have no image of It, nor do I know Its needs. Think of those last six words for a moment: I do not know the needs of the *I* that I am.

At the moment, I may think of some needs, but they are not *My* needs: they are the needs of somebody I have built up in my own mind, somebody living a so-called human life. If I am wholly on the spiritual path, I must have passed the stage of praying for anything of a human nature, knowing full well that if I should get it, it might bring trouble with it or prove unsatisfying after it arrived.

"I and my Father are one," but I do not know what the Father is. I do not know what the I *is, but I do know that* I *am; and in that* I *that I am is included, through Grace, all of which I shall have need unto eternity. I and my Father being one,* I *is that very God; not the God to whom I pray for things, but rather the God who knows what things I have need of. Furthermore, it is* I's *good pleasure to give me the Kingdom.*

I *in the midst of me is omniscience and knows all things of which I have need.* I *in the midst of me is omnipotence and has the power to provide whatever is necessary.* I *is the omnipresent love, and it is the good pleasure of this* I *in the midst of me to give me that which It already knows is my need.*

What words could follow that? How could you go any further than that in prayer? The moment you prayed for any thing or any condition, you would be making a laughingstock of God. *I* in the midst of you, then, is the fulfillment of all your dreams, because you and the Father are one and in that oneness is fulfillment. There is not *I,* the Father, and I, the son. *I* the Father and I the son are one; and therefore, in the presence of the *I* that you are is your fulfillment.

The Nature of I

All discord, all inharmony, and all error are experienced because of a sense of separation from God. But this sense of separation from God is not your fault personally. It is the universal belief that has come down to us from the allegorical experience of Adam and Eve being cast out of the Garden of Eden. Nevertheless, this universal sense of separation from God is responsible for our sins, diseases, death, lack, and limitation. Therefore, immortality and infinity can be returned to us only as we return to the Father's house.

This means to realize that what you are looking at with your eyes is not *I*: *I* am invisible; *I* am omnipresence; *I* am omnipotence; *I* am omniscience. You prove this by not taking thought, by being still, and by letting the Omniscience that *I* am reveal to you whatever wisdom, guidance, or direction is necessary at this moment. You prove this by being still in the listening attitude, letting Omnipotence prove Itself to be the only power. You prove this by taking no thought for your life or anything that concerns your life, and letting Omnipresence prove Omnipresence.

This cannot be done intellectually. It can be done only through unknowing, through silence. Silence is your resting place. Silence is your abiding place, your living place. Live and move and have your being in silence, and then the still small voice will utter itself and live your life.

The moment you take thought you are living your own life, and your life then becomes limited to a certain measure of education, environment, circumstances, and conditions. As long as you have no graven image of God in your thought, not praying to a far-off or close-at-hand God, as long as you are abiding in *I*—*I,* Omniscience, *I,* Omnipresence, *I,* Omnipotence—then by the grace of God your needs are met.

Now, as of old, the danger is that you will pray for material things or desire material things, which means that you would like God, Spirit, to fulfill your concepts rather than to express God's way and God's will. To pray and have in mind anything or any condition that you want from God is to create the barrier separating you from it, because there is no God separate and apart from you, and that "you" has no problems.

I and my Father have no problems. I and my Father are incorporeal, spiritual. I and my Father are truth. In this right identity, His word goes before me to "make the crooked places straight." His word that knows my need fulfills it.

Do you not see that setting up an "I" with some problem, with some desire, with some need to be fulfilled is setting up a selfhood apart from God? Do you not see that this is a denial of the Master's teaching?

I and the Father have no problems. I and the Father are not immature or aged: I and my Father are ageless. "Before Abraham was, I am. . . . I will never leave thee. . . . I am with you alway, even unto the end of the world."

I—but do not have any picture in your mind when you say *"I,"* because when I speak of *I,* I am not speaking of a man, not of a man two thousand years ago nor of a man today. I am speaking of *I,* and no one—not you, not I—can possibly know what *I* looks like. Be assured, however, that *I* and my Father are one, not two, and that One is hid with Christ in God; that One lives, moves, and has Its being in the Divine.

Imparting I

I in the midst of you is mighty, but the moment you create an image, you have *I and* an image. Therefore, do not have any "I" but the *I* that you declare: *I.* Be satisfied with the word *I.* Some day you will hear the Voice say to you, *"I,"* and when It does you will know that you have come face to face with God. You have come to know God aright. But you will not be able to tell your neighbor about it, or your child, your husband, your wife, or your parents, because that would be trying to bring *I* down to the intellect again, down to the mind.

If I succeed in imparting *I* to you through this work, it will be because I have realized that I am not a man or a teacher, but that I am divine Presence; and also because you have been drawn to this work by *I* to receive *I,* to receive the unveiling of the *I* which you are. Both of these are necessary.

In writing of the unveiling of God, the unveiling of Truth, you might think that there is a God that could be unveiled and set before you. Such is not the case. The "unveiling" reveals nothing that can be seen, heard, tasted, touched, or smelled, nothing that can be thought or reasoned, and therefore it should not seem strange that in order to know Him aright you must come to a place in consciousness where you know nothing, the place of unknowing.

I, *the Identity of Every Person*

Perhaps all of us in the past have loved mother, brother, or child more than *Me,* more than Truth. This has been a barrier. Why? Because that mother, brother, sister, or child to whom we were clinging was not mother, brother, sister, or child but an image that we were carrying in our mind which we believed needed us.

Once you recognize *I* as the identity of yourself, you will recognize It as the identity of mother, brother, sister, and child, and then you can have no fear of releasing them into their God-identity. The Master never meant that you should abandon your family, but merely urged you to go up higher in your awareness of what constitutes your family, and ultimately to realize that God is your only family.

When you realize that God is your mother, brother, sister, or father, that God is your husband, your wife, your child, the one *I,* the one Life, then all fear for them goes, and when fear goes you have released them into their true identity, into God. Your love for them is greater; their love for you is greater; the bond is greater; and the need is less because each finds fulfillment from the divine Center within.

I *Is Omniscience, Omnipotence, and Omnipresence*

For many of us it has been easy to accept God as Omnipotence, Omniscience, and Omnipresence, not knowing that we were leaving ourselves locked out in the blizzard. But *I* is that omnipotence; *I* is that omniscience; *I* is that omnipresence. Abide in this word *I.*

Whether you say that God is omniscience, omnipotence, and omnipresence or that Jesus is omnipotence, omniscience, and omnipresence really makes no difference, because in either case you have set up God and Jesus as separate and apart from the Self which you are, the *I* which you are. When, however, you bring it all down to *I* and the Father are one, and know that *I* is omniscience, *I* is omnipotence, *I* is omnipresence, in this oneness you are infinite in being. In this oneness, the *I* of you is immortality. Then you will see what a difference this makes in the nature of your daily life.

You are demonstrating the presence of God every time you realize *I.* Close your eyes, turn within with a listening ear, and God will reveal Itself. God will reveal His presence in the midst of you, but you must open out a way: you must empty the vessels already full; you must enter into the silence with no concepts.

It is as if you were asked to draw a picture of Mars and you would have to say, "How can I? I've never seen Mars." Good, then turn within, because you may be assured that Omniscience, the mind of God, knows what Mars is like and will reveal it to you if there should be any occasion for you to know about it.

Nothing is hidden from the mind of God, which is the mind of man. Any legitimate need of any nature that ever appears in your experience can be immediately fulfilled as long as you do not think of it as a material form. Think of it as the grace of God, the omniscience of God, the omnipotence of God, the omnipresence of God, the spirit of God in man, and then let That take whatever form It will.

Imagery Can Become a Barrier

You cannot expect miracles simply by intellectually saying, "I and my Father are one." But you can accept that statement of truth and then go within until the Father confirms it within you. He says, "Yes, indeed, *I* am you. *I* am the only 'you' there is. *I* am all there is to you. You are nothing but *I*." And if you recall how many times during one day you use the word "I," you will know that this is absolute truth. All there is to you is *I*—only not the limited sense of "I" that you entertain of yourself, but the *I* that you really are, the child of God, one with the Father.

Probably the very fact that the Master was a Hebrew helped to set up this sense of separation between the Father and His individualization, because Jesus used the Hebrew imagery of father and child, and that always makes us think of a great wise parent and a little immature child: twoness. In fact, we cannot conceive of a parent and child being one. We see the parent and the child, and we know they are two. Even while the child is being carried in the mother's womb, the child and the mother are still two, the child something separate and apart from the mother. So this very imagery that was used in ancient Hebrew teaching can be a barrier, and it is sometimes necessary to get away from that image of father and child and cling only to *I, I, I. I* and truth are one. *I* and life are one.

The Birthless and Deathless I

There is a passage in the Bhagavad-Gita that is rarely understood and sometimes very harshly criticized.

> He who shall say, "Lo! I have slain a man!"
> He who shall think, "Lo! I am slain!" those both
> Know naught! Life cannot slay. Life is not slain!
> Never the spirit was born; the spirit shall cease to be never;
> Never was time it was not; End and Beginning are dreams!*

This almost seems as if Krishna, who is speaking, were condoning murder, but it does not mean that. It means that *I* cannot be slain, and *I* cannot slay. Then what about the person who is slain or does the slaying? Ah, no! Life is never slain, and that is where true identity comes in: *I* am not the body that is buried. *I* am the life that is continuous, and that life which *I* am is never slain. That life which *I* am, even as the life of the one I slay, is not slain. We look at the fallen body and we forget that *I* is not the body, and the body is not *I. I* is infinite, incorporeal spiritual being. Regardless of what you do or do not do to the body, *I* remain forever and forever and forever. There is no end to the *I* that I am. "I will never leave thee, nor forsake thee. . . . I am with you alway, even unto the end of the world," and that is the *I* that you declare.

If you think for a minute that Jesus or any other mystic is referring

* *The Song Celestial,* Edwin Arnold, trans. (Philadelphia: David McKay Co.).

to himself when he speaks of *I,* you are in error, because when the Master said "I," he meant *I,* the *I* that is the *I* in the midst of you. And that gives meaning to one of the greatest passages of Scripture: "I am come that they might have life, and that they might have it more abundantly." If you remember that that passage refers to *I* in the midst of you, never again will you fear for your life, for your supply, for your happiness, or for your security. It is to this *I* that is in the midst of you that you must always look, and to no other. Let the divine *I* live your life by living consciously in the *I* in the midst of you, the *I* that you declare is come that you might have life infinitely, abundantly, immortally, and eternally.

CHAPTER IV

"I AM THE WAY"

One of the most important statements in the New Testament is the passage, "I am the way." The incorrect interpretation of these few words has kept the world in spiritual darkness for seventeen hundred years. On his understanding of that one passage hinges man's spiritual darkness or his spiritual enlightenment. That same passage of Scripture correctly interpreted, however, can set the world free, but to accomplish this there must be the "ten righteous men" to show forth the correct understanding of the passage by their fruitage. The fruitage of spiritual enlightenment is freedom, peace, abundance—all that the Master meant to convey when he said, "I am come that they might have life, and that they might have it more abundantly."

When you personalize these words of Jesus and believe that they refer to a person, you are in spiritual darkness. Did not Jesus say, "I can of mine own self do nothing. . . . If I bear witness of myself, my witness is not true"? Think of the degree of spiritual ignorance in which a person lives when he worships and prays to someone who frankly, openly, and honestly declares, "I can of mine own self do nothing. . . . If I bear witness of myself, my witness is not true"!

Rightly interpreted, the words "I am the way" mean what they say. The way, the truth, and the life more abundant are to be found in *I*—the *I* that I am, the *I* that you are, for you have been told that you and your Father are one. It is in that oneness that you find spiritual freedom, spiritual harmony, and spiritual grace, a life "not by might, nor by power, but by my spirit."

I is the way, and that way reveals that "I and my Father are one. . . . I will never leave thee, nor forsake thee. . . . I am with you alway, even unto the end of the world." It is in this word *I* that you find the entire secret of the spiritual message given to the world by Christ Jesus, a message that is destined to set men free and break from them all shackles and all limitations, that they may live as children of God, completely free, under the domination of no man, under the domination of no circumstances or conditions, and under the grace of God alone. When this is translated into practical life experience, you will begin to understand some of the passages of Scripture that have heretofore been obscure.

He That Is Within You Is Greater

Consider this passage: "Greater is he that is in you, than he that is in the world." Who is this He that is within you that is greater than he that is in the world? Is there any He within you other than the *I* of your own being, your own Self? Is there another? Think of these words: "The Father that dwelleth in me, he doeth the works." Who is this Father within? Does it not mean that there is a Presence within you, and a Power as well, since He performs that which is given you to do? This He that is within you does those things appointed for you to do.

"Fear not, for I am with thee." Can you agree within yourself that this "Fear not, for I am with thee" refers to a Presence, a Power, and a Wisdom? Fear not! "It is I; be not afraid." How can you help but fear unless there is Omnipotence, Omnipresence, Omniscience? "It is I; be not afraid. . . . Fear not, for I am with thee."

Do not these words reveal that there is a Presence within you, a Power, and a Wisdom? Whether we accept the Master's designation of that Presence, Power, and Wisdom as *I* or as the Father within, or whether it is easier for us to go along with Paul's statement, "I can do all things through Christ which strengtheneth me," through the Christ that dwells in us, the truth is that that Spirit—that Presence, that Power, that Wisdom—is within each and every one of us.

Spirit Is the Creator of All Being

There is an indwelling Presence in you, in me, and in everyone, and since Jesus' message was addressed to saints and sinners alike, it must also apply to saints and sinners alike now. Since it was addressed to Hebrews first and Christians later, it must apply equally to Hebrews, Christians, and all others who hear this Word, who hear that they are not to be afraid because *I* within is the Christ, the Presence, the Power, the Wisdom. "Be still, and know that I am God." Is that *I* a man, or is It this Presence, Power, and Wisdom within you? "Choose you this day whom ye will serve"—a man or *I?*

Until you can arrive at this recognition and conviction and until you come to an inner assurance that there is this He within you, this *I,* because of Whom you need not fear, you can go no further and your tomorrows will be no different from your yesterdays. Do not try to go beyond this moment of revelation regardless of how many months or years it may take for you to reach the absolute inner conviction:

Where I am, God is. I need never fear; I need never be afraid. This Presence is with me. This I *is within me.*

Without this realized Presence, you are the man of earth who is not under the law of God, and you do not receive the things of God. It is only when you come to the absolute conviction that the Spirit of God is with you and that the Spirit of God goes where you go that you are fulfilling the promise that those who have the Spirit of God are children of God, heirs of God, "joint-heirs with Christ" to all the heavenly riches. But whether or not you acknowledge or recognize It, the Spirit of God is always and ever with you, even though It is of no avail to you, because it is only through your awareness of It, your consciousness of Its presence, that It functions.

The Spirit of God is within me and dwells in me. The Spirit of God goes before me to "make the crooked places straight," to prepare mansions for me. The Spirit of God has ordained me.

Only when you have come into this agreement within yourself do you become the child of God. Then you no longer live by effort, but by Grace. You then inherit your good. You do not labor for it, struggle for it, strive for it: you inherit it.

Prayer Becomes an Inner Communion

This in no wise means that you enter a life of indolence, because once the Spirit of God is upon you, you are called upon to fulfill God's mission for you, and that entails more work than you may have dreamed of. But now it no longer involves striving or struggling, and no longer is there a seeking for things. This is the miracle, the miracle that changes your entire concept of prayer, for you no longer pray for the things of this world. You no longer pray for happiness, for security, or for peace on earth. Your prayer now is a continuous inner communion with that Spirit which you have acknowledged.

In other words, the nature of prayer is changed. No longer do you take thought for anything that concerns your human life, because with the assurance of this inner Presence and Its promise to give you the life more abundant, you have nothing more to do with the outer plane of life than to accept God's grace as It flows into and through your experience, and quite naturally compels you to share the twelve baskets full with those who have not yet realized that there is no use struggling for full baskets. The only struggle, and it is not a struggle, should be for the awareness that *I,* the Spirit of God, is within you. The full baskets will appear of their own accord. There is no use in struggling for health even through prayer or treatment, once you have realized that the function of the Spirit of God in you is to give you health abundantly.

As long as you live constantly and consciously in this truth of the indwelling Presence and Its function in your life and in the life of your friends and enemies, you are living a life of prayer. You are living the contemplative life: contemplating God, contemplating the presence of His son within you. See what this does for you. Every time you think of the son of God, you no longer think back two thousand years to Galilee. Now, whenever you think of the son of God, you immediately realize that you are speaking of the son of God who dwells in you, the Christ that dwelt in Paul years after the Crucifixion.

All there is to a spiritually fruitful life is this conscious abiding in and through the Presence. "I can do all things." Does that mean that I am so great? No, I can do all things because His Spirit dwells in me, and It voices Itself over and over and over again saying, "Fear not, *I* am with you. Be not afraid, *I* am with you. *I* will never leave you."

This is the presence of God that has spoken to me and is now speaking to you from within you after you have pondered this truth of Scripture that *I* is the way. The presence of *I* in you is really the way. When you raise up the son of God in you, you hear, "*I* will never leave you. *I* am come that you might have life and have a more abundant life."

Seek the Reality and Not the Shadow

When you have so raised up this son of God in you, you are the child of God, and you live not by taking thought for your life, "not by might, nor by power," but by this indwelling Spirit. Never again is it possible to be tempted to accept the belief that you must demonstrate anything other than the continuous realization of this indwelling Presence, because It becomes the form of fulfillment.

I dare not pray for success, for any success separate and apart from the presence of God would be for me failure. Only in the realization of the presence of God can I find success. True, when that success appears, it appears outwardly in tangible form as students, messages, books, or whatever it is that is intended for this experience.

I dare not pray for supply because any supply separate and apart from God would not be supply at all: it would be a shadow; it would be an image; it would be something false, certainly nothing to rely upon. But, as I confine my prayer to this realization of God's presence, or God's grace, It appears tangibly and outwardly in the form necessary: sometimes pounds, dollars, marks, or francs, sometimes publishers, sometimes recognition in other forms, sometimes transportation. Always the realized Presence appears as the form necessary to the fulfillment of that moment.

Do you see then why the Master cautioned against praying for food, clothing, and housing? Do you see why he cautioned against taking thought for those things? Seek the realization of this Presence; seek only within your own consciousness for the constant remembrance.

> I *am with thee. Rest; abide in that Word. Abide in that consciousness. Fear not, be not afraid;* I *am with thee.* I *will never leave thee.* I *will be with thee until the end of the world.* My *presence goes before thee.*

Abide in this Word, and then this Spirit of God will appear to you in the form of fulfillment for your life, and in some other form of fulfillment for my life. For both of us it will be fulfillment, and yet the forms may differ, since what represents fulfillment to you may not represent fulfillment to me. Furthermore, what represents fulfillment today may not represent fulfillment a year from now. As you remember that it is the recognition of the presence of God in you, and as you are still enough to recognize the presence of this *I* within you, It then takes care of the daily bread, food, clothing, housing, joy, peace, safety, security, reward, and recognition—whatever the nature of the fulfillment is to be.

You cannot afford to accept these two points and go on as if you had read a beautiful lesson. You must take them into your consciousness for a day, a week, a month, or a year if necessary, until they have come to fruition within you, and you yourself have attained an understanding of the nature of the revelation of Jesus Christ that *I* is the way. Through *I,* which is the divine Presence within you, you are fulfilled. Through this *I* which is God within you, through This you live. This is the way of life, and you live through this Presence: in It, with It, through It, by It. Commune with It. Live and move and have your being in It and with It. Be still and know *I.* Be still and hear the still small voice say to you, "Fear not, *I* am with you. Be not afraid, *I* am He."

Rest in Me

Then you will know that the miracle of the Christian life is that *I,* God, in the midst of you am omnipotence. Rest in *Me.* Rest in *My* word. Rest in that word *I* in the midst of you. Rest in that presence of God. Rest in the assurance of Its presence and of Its mission. Abide in It. Never take anxious thought, worrisome thought, or fearful thought for the things of this world.

Take all the thought you wish in doing your work correctly, perfectly, with timeliness, and lovingly. Take much thought about being neighborly to your friends and to your enemies, and take thought about praying for those enemies. Take thought about forgiving seventy times seven, but take no thought for your own life, for this is the function of the *I* that dwells in you. *I* is the way. Be not afraid, it is *I;* and then relax in that *I.* Relax in that Presence. Relax in that Power. Relax in the assurance that *I* is something that will never leave you nor forsake you.

This *I* will not keep you on earth forever, for that is not Its function. Its function is that you live forever, but not necessarily in England or the United States, France, Germany, or Switzerland, or anywhere on earth. It should make no difference where you live as long as you live by the grace of God. Here, there, or any other place should be the same to you.

Entering the Inner Sanctuary

I is never a person. It is not my person or your person. *I* is always the divine Selfhood, the Creator, the Word that is in the midst of you. When you recognize It, you are living the Christian way, the way of *I,* the way of the indwelling Presence, the way of prayer and communion, entering the inner sanctuary of your own being to find God.

As you read the Bible, you may believe that the inner sanctuary or holy of holies that the Hebrew priests entered was an edifice. This is merely a way of presenting it, but it has a much deeper inner meaning. There never has been an edifice erected that was the holy of holies—not even King Solomon's temple in Jerusalem. It too went the way of all flesh. All material structures go that way. The holy of holies is your consciousness, the inner sanctuary of your own being. You are never in the holy of holies until you have gone within yourself and there found God, tabernacled with Him, spoken to Him, and heard God—all within yourself.

"Whither shall I go from thy spirit?" Here where I am, God is, and I need only turn from material edifices, material kingdoms, and retire within to the spiritual edifice, the temple not made with hands, to My *kingdom, the*

spiritual kingdom, and there, within the temple of my own being, within this invisible, spiritual sanctuary which my consciousness is, I can hear the voice of God. There I can bear witness as It utters Its voice. I can hear the still small voice, and I can watch the earth of error—sin, disease, lack, limitation —crumble as this Voice says, "Be not afraid, it is I. *Fear not,* I *am with thee."*

Remember consciously when you awaken in the morning that where you are is this temple of God. As you go about your business during the day, whether you find yourself in your home, your office, on the street, in a bus, or in trouble, turn within and realize: "I am the temple of God, and God dwells in me, in this temple here where I am."

Practice this presence of God in you. Practice it morning, noon, and night, under any circumstance and every circumstance, but more especially those that appear to be evil circumstances. Pray the prayer of remembrance—not a prayer for things you need or want or should have, but the prayer of remembrance: Be not afraid, it is *I*. Be still and know that *I* within you am God.

CHAPTER V

THE TWO WAYS OF I

Those of you who are on the spiritual path are living in two worlds, the material and the spiritual. It may be that some of you at the moment are experiencing very little of the spiritual world, but surely you do occasionally catch glimpses of it in or after a meditation. The experience of this expanded consciousness may come, too, when you have asked for help, have been temporarily lifted out of yourself—out of your problems or out of your body—and for a brief second have caught a glimpse of a consciousness beyond that of the "natural man," the man who never enters heaven, never receives a blessing from God, and is never under the law of God. The consciousness of the natural man is just a branch of a tree that is cut off and is withering, gradually approaching threescore years and ten—a few more or a few less—never even suspecting that there is another realm.

While in the consciousness of the natural man, something within turns you in the direction of a spiritual teaching, and if this teaching happens to be The Infinite Way, you are led not merely through some principles of metaphysics, but into the practice of principles that must eventually result in meditation. It is in meditation that this glimpse of the spiritual kingdom is given to you, because in meditation you are not seeking things. You are not seeking health, prosperity, or companionship: you are seeking the kingdom of God, and "in such an hour as ye think not the Son of man cometh," the Christ reveals Itself, and spiritual Grace takes over. It might be a momentary glimpse which leaves you for days and does not return, but if you are really determined to follow this path you will keep at it until that awareness does return, not once but again and again. The more often you seek it and the more often you attain it, the closer you are to that place where you are living more in the kingdom of God than in the world.

The Light Is Given to Be a Light

Sometimes people think that in coming into the spiritual life they are going to leave the business world. This is rarely true, because they take upon their shoulders the instruction of students, healing work, and all the business affairs that are connected with a spiritual ministry.

Even in a spiritual activity, you will find yourself in a measure involved in the business world, and some of it may be pleasant and some of it not so pleasant. Some of the teaching work is very pleasant, and some of it is not. But you yourself will have arrived at the place where you are living more and more in the spiritual realm and less and less in the world, and whether pleasant or unpleasant, it will make no difference to you.

With every person who has attained a measure of light, a grave question arises: "Has God been so good to me as to give me this spiritual light and all the great spiritual blessings that have come to me even on the human plane for my benefit only? Has He done that for me? Does He want to set me up as His special child to receive special favors so that the rest of the world can say, 'Oh, isn't he fortunate? He has God's grace.' "

Then the answer begins to come to him: "Heavens, no! I have not been permitted to receive all this for me. This is only that I may be a light unto those still in darkness. This has not been given to me for me at all."

As a matter of fact, my own experience has been that the further I go, the less use I have of all this good that has come to me because I am so busy with the work, and so I know that this has not been given to me to give me leisure which has never come, but rather to make me a light that may illumine those still in darkness and those who are still seeking.

In the beginning, you become a light to some members of your family, your neighbors, friends, or fellow students, but eventually you realize that that is not enough. God did not place the sun in the heavens for one person alone. It is there for both the saints and the sinners; it is for all alike. God did not send Jesus into the world just for the Hebrews of the Holy Land, nor just for the Christians who became the followers of the disciples; but rather that the spiritual message of the Master should become universal, and that the mind that was in Christ Jesus might become the mind of man.

"I" Can Do Nothing, but I *Within Can Do All Things*

Jesus said, "I can of mine own self do nothing. . . . If I bear witness of myself, my witness is not true." Now you must pause for a moment and ponder that because, as you read the New Testament, you will not have to read very far until you hear him say, "He that seeth me seeth him that sent me. . . . I and my Father are one. . . . I am the way, the truth, and the life. . . . I am the light of the world. . . . I am come that they might have life." All this will cause you to be very careful about the use of the word "I," so that you watch what you are doing when you use that word.

The message of The Infinite Way is making clear that which has been lost to the church for seventeen hundred years, the truth that there is a human "I" who can do nothing, and there is a divine *I* within you through which you can do all things.

You must know that there is an "I" called Joel and there is an "I" called you. But neither you nor Joel has fully attained: Joel is likely to make mistakes; Joel might sometime or other get very angry; Joel at times enjoys a good meal. But this is not the *I* that is the spiritual teacher or revelator. This is the part of my selfhood which is still in personal sense, and it is the one of which Jesus spoke when he said, "I can of mine own self do nothing."

Once you make this same acknowledgment, you can then say, "Ah, but my Selfhood, my real Selfhood, is divine. My Savior, my Christ, my Healer, my Supplier is closer to me than the breathing within me. It is the very *I* of my being." When you have recognized this, you begin to withdraw your faith, hope, and confidence in the external world and in human beings. You will do your best to be led spiritually when you go to the polls to vote, but you will not put your dependence for freedom and peace on whoever is elected, whether it is your candidate or the other person's candidate. You will be living consciously in the awareness of this *I* within you. This is praying without ceasing, constantly realizing that *I* in the midst of you is mighty. *I* in the midst of you is the bread, the meat, the wine, and the water of your life.

The Separation

All this leads us to a very difficult place in our journey. We are so accustomed to read and hear the beautiful biblical promises of a perfect heaven that we sometimes forget there are also some other biblical promises which we may have overlooked: "Strait is the gate, and narrow is the way, which leadeth unto life, and few there be that find it. . . . I came not to send peace, but a sword. For I am come to set a man at variance against his father, and the daughter against her mother, and the daughter in law against her mother in law."

We skim over those passages as if they were not important or not intended to be taken seriously. Of course, they are not meant to be taken literally, but be assured that Jesus meant what he said, because the division is taking place, and it is taking place the very moment that you begin to rely on the *I* within you and not on your parents, children, aunts, uncles, or cousins. A division has occurred right there: you are being separated from your dependence on persons.

As long as there are two states of consciousness—the material and the spiritual—you will find that there will be a division or separation from those of your relatives who prefer to remain in material consciousness, even if they are your own children or parents. You may not move out of their home or put them out of your home, but there will be a wall between you—a wall that means a lack of understanding. And you will really find that your companionship, your wholeness and oneness, will be with those of your spiritual household rather than with those of your family household. To that extent, there will be a separation or division. Such experiences often take people from the spiritual path. As the Master said, "Few there be that find it." Scripture also says, "For many are called, but few are chosen."

Making the Transition to Spiritual Consciousness

If you examine your thoughts honestly, you will discover that the reason for your approach, at least your first or earliest approach, to a metaphysical or spiritual work was the desire for the improvement of human conditions, and nothing more nor less than that. It was a way to achieve better health, better supply, or better companionship, and now to your surprise or dismay you are faced with the fact that just the opposite may take place. You may lose some of your companions, some of your friendships.

In the same way, in seeking health, sometimes when you are hoping to get rid of one undesirable condition, you may discover that you have three or four others along with that one. They have been latent in your body or mind, and now this stirs them up, and all of a sudden you discover ailments you never knew you had. At first you might think that your spiritual study brought this on. No, your spiritual study did not bring it on, but it did bring to the surface whatever was latent in mind or body, and the right attitude is to be grateful, because otherwise it would lie dormant there until it got ready to strike; whereas now at least it has come to the surface, and through your study and work you will have the opportunity to make a transition from a material sense of health to the spiritual consciousness of wholeness.

It is possible that in your early metaphysical life you were satisfied to have an unpleasant condition changed into a pleasant one, an unhealthy body into a healthy one, or a lacking purse into an abundant one. But as you remain on the spiritual path this will no longer satisfy you, because you will discover that there does come an end to all material good, whether of the body or of the purse; and therefore, in trying to avoid making the transition to spiritual wholeness and completeness, you will know that you have merely postponed the ills of the flesh or of the purse.

So, eventually, you come to that place where through spiritual consciousness you rise above the idea of good health, good supply, and good companionship. As you live in this consciousness and as you stop rejoicing in physical health, material wealth, or human happiness, always turning within and remembering that all this is but the outer manifestation of an inner grace, you are making the transition to a health which is not of the body but of the Soul, and to the point where supply is not money, but it has its source in the Soul.

The only way this can be accomplished is by the realization that *I,* the wine of inspiration, the bread of life, is the source of spiritual harmony appearing outwardly as human good. During this transitional period, you are continuously going within for the remembrance of this indwelling *I,* this Christ, this Self. We call this practicing the presence of God, realizing God, God-realization, or Self-realization. All these terms mean the same thing. They mean that you are realizing that there is more to you than you can see in the mirror, that there is an invisible Something that is the most important part of your life and of your being, because the invisible part is the source of the visible.

Love and Joy, the Fruitage of Contemplation

In meditation, you contemplate the spiritual activity and being that is within yourself. You contemplate God's grace which is established within you, and acknowledge that God has planted His son in you, that God is your only Father, and therefore that your inheritance is of the Father and not by virtue of being good, since it comes to saint and sinner alike when readiness has established it. This is living the contemplative life, contemplating always the Infinite Invisible of your being, that Christhood of your being, that divine *I* within, and knowing that that very *I* is come that you might have life and have it more abundantly. Such a contemplation brings a dropping away of love, hate, and fear of the external world. You say, "Do you stop loving it?" Unduly loving it, yes, or perhaps you stop loving it in the wrong way and begin to love it in the right way.

Too much of what the world calls love is based on a love for some person's body. All the satisfaction some people get comes from someone's body or from someone's purse. But that is not loving in the right way. That kind of love proves very unsatisfying and comes to an end. But when an individual begins to realize that this invisible Presence within himself is really the Soul of husband, wife, child, friend, and neighbor, then they begin to perceive that same Soul in him, and the love takes on an entirely different nature. The animal part of it goes, and a joy comes in.

Going from Humanhood to Christhood

So it is, then, that in these two worlds there is always a "you" communing with the invisible Presence which Jesus called the Father within, and which Paul called the Christ. Actually it is the Spirit in man. The same Spirit "that raised up Christ from the dead shall also quicken your mortal bodies." Now where is that same Spirit that raised up Jesus Christ from the dead? Is it in the Holy Land of two thousand years ago, or do you have to go to the Holy Land for it now? No, the same Spirit that raised up Jesus Christ from the dead is within you. You do not get It: you acknowledge It, recognize It, and let It flow. It is your dwelling in the consciousness of Its presence, your acknowledging Its presence within you, your communing in your silent moments with It that brings It more and more into manifestation.

It was in such moments of conscious oneness with God that Jesus could say, "He that seeth me seeth him that sent me. . . . I and my Father are one." In that elevated consciousness, Jesus was absent, and only God, the divine *I,* was present and speaking. When he says, "I am come that they might have life, and that they might have it more abundantly," he is speaking not as a man, but as God: he has risen above his manhood into his Godhood.

There are those who through this communion eventually attain the ultimate experience which is conscious union with God, and who rise above their manhood and womanhood into their Godhood. As with the Master, it is not, however, a continuous experience that goes on for the rest of one's life. It is an intermittent one—here today and gone tomorrow. There were times when Jesus was so downcast that he wanted to go away for forty days or so downhearted that he had to ask the disciples to pray with him. Certainly Jesus was not in his Godhood in that moment in Gethsemane when he asked the disciples to stay awake with him, and he expected that their prayers would lift him up.

In Meditation, Climb into Your I*-ness*

Our meditations for one another, and even what we call treatment, are not for the purpose of healing disease or lack. They are for the purpose of lifting the student up out of his manhood and womanhood into his Christhood, where there is no sin, disease, death, lack, or limitation. When you are abiding in your Christhood, you can look out and say, "What did hinder you?" because you do not see any reason why even the paralyzed cannot walk. It is in your Christhood that you can command the blind to open their eyes. This you cannot do in your humanhood, because nothing happens. Most healing work actually takes place when the practitioner, through deep meditation, has lifted himself out of his humanhood into his Christhood. The more years a person works as a practitioner and spiritual teacher, the more hours of the day or the night he is in his Christhood and therefore the fewer specific treatments he has to give.

That brings us to an important part of Infinite Way meditation. Never do we direct thought outside to a person or a condition. The directing of thought is entirely a mental process. The object of it is really suggestion. This is not to say that some persons are not healed through suggestion, for they are. What we are saying is that that is no part of Infinite Way practice, because it violates one of the basic principles of The Infinite Way.

The human mind can be used for good and evil, and the human mind can make honest mistakes. Therefore, we do not want the human mind to enter into our spiritual practice or our relationship with our students. In meditation, the personal "I" which is Joel or the personal "I" of any practitioner must cease to function, because no one has the right to believe that he has the power to give a person anything. If he did have, where would God come in? After more than thirty years of this practice, no one knows better than I do that "silver and gold have I none"—that things of the world have I none to give.

There is only one thing that I have or any real spiritual teacher has, and that is an understanding of the nature of *I,* of the infinite invisible Selfhood. Therefore, when I meditate for you or with you, I do not permit you to enter my mind, and I do not project myself into your mind. What I do is to close my eyes and climb right into my *I*-ness. I want to commune and be one with this *I* that I am, and with a listening ear and my attention centered on the Infinite Invisible, I am still. Then the Spirit of God is loosed, and because a person has brought himself to my consciousness, he receives the fruitage.

Let us see how it operates. There may be a person who is physically ill, and because of my retiring within into that *I*-ness, that stillness, my being still and knowing that *I* is God and letting that *I* be God, this person can receive a physical healing. But another can receive a moral healing, another a financial healing, and yet another employment or a healing of human relationships. Yet I know nothing about this at all.

When you reach out to any individual whom you recognize to be God-realized, this recognition of the Christ of his being is an indication of your receptivity, and that is what gives you the benefit of his meditation. You do not even have to be in the physical presence of such a person to benefit by the *I* that he is. The Master said, "Thy faith hath made thee whole"—thy faith, thy recognition.

"Whom say ye that I am?" *I* is God. If you recognize that *I* is God when you turn to a practitioner, you cannot help being benefited. But if you think that the practitioner has the power to give you something, withhold something, or delay it, or if you think that money has the power to buy it, you are missing the way. Money is a tool; it can be used as an expression of gratitude, and in that sense it is an acknowledgment, but it is not going to purchase anything. The only thing that will purchase anything of a spiritual nature is your recognition of, and your contact with, one who has attained some measure of Christ-life, some realization of the Christ of his being, of the nature of the *I* that he is.

Gaining Our Freedom by Losing Our Human Sense of Identity in I

When you understand that Jesus used the word "I" in two different ways, you will begin to perceive that the secret of his mission was to reveal that *I* is God, the *I* that is in the midst of you, the *I* which is the very nature and character of your own being. You are really the son of God in your spiritual identity, and this outer self that calls itself Mary, Jim, or Joel is the prodigal working his way back to the Father's house until eventually he does not repeat his given name any more: he says, *"I."*

In one way or another, we all lose the sense of attachment that has made us proud to belong to this family or that family, or to this country or that country, this race or that race, this religion or that religion. We lose it all in proportion to the realization of that word *I,* because the *I* of me is the *I* of you. If there is only one Father in heaven, you and I are brothers and sisters, and the sooner we awaken to this and begin to act like it, the sooner we bring about our own emancipation and the freedom of those who come within range of our consciousness.

Through the realization of the Infinite Invisible within you, you attain your freedom from this world. You will not lose your love for your parents or your children, but it will be love of a different nature. You will not be a slave to it, and you will not hold them in bondage to it. Then, too, you will probably contribute more money for benevolence and charity in the world, and yet have less sympathy and pity than ever before, because even while you are helping your fellow man at his level of consciousness, you will realize that he does not have to be poor or enslaved. Poverty and enslavement are states of ignorance. Anyone who awakens to the nature of *I,* his true identity, must become free—free of sin, free of disease, free of lack.

If, when you close your eyes in prayer or meditation, you are thinking of people, please remember that you may be transferring good or evil to them—sometimes evil under the name of good. But if you really want to be a blessing to this world, to your family, to your neighbors, or to your students, do not allow human thinking to enter your mind, because that is the thinking of the little "I," and sometimes with even the best of intentions it could be wrong. Be still and know that *I* in the midst of you am God, and let that *I* do the work. Then the message or the help that your friend, relative, patient, or student gets will be directly from God. It will be the Spirit Itself bearing witness with your spirit, and there will be harmony and peace.

CHAPTER VI

IMPERSONALIZING GOD

If someone were to ask you, "What is this Infinite Way? What is there about it that holds your interest and apparently benefits you?" you would probably have a difficult time answering, because what holds and benefits you and is your Comforter is something you know with your fourth-dimensional Consciousness, and if you should try to impart it to someone still living in the third-dimensional or material state of consciousness, he would never understand what you were attempting to tell him.

In trying to explain this you might say, "Oh, I have learned that evil is not power," and then, of course, you would be ridiculed. If you said, "I have discovered God," you would then be asked to explain that, and anyone who has ever been called upon to tell what he has found out about God knows how foolish it would be to try. No one can do that, because whatever it is you may know about God you do not know with your mind. To have any awareness of God means that you have already broken through the area of mind and have been lifted into the higher consciousness. Whatever you may know about God, you know through your spiritual awareness, through your developed spiritual discernment, through the Soul-faculties. To try to tell this to a person living out from a materialistic consciousness would be nonsensical, if not impossible.

Universality and Availability of the Mind That Was in Christ Jesus

The Infinite Way begins with the revelation that there is a transcendental consciousness, which in Christian mysticism is called Christ-consciousness and in Buddhism is called the Buddha-mind. In either case, what is meant is that there is a consciousness higher than the human mind. This is not a matter of general knowledge. True, there may be those who accept the idea that Buddha had that spiritual consciousness and that Jesus had the mind that was in Christ, but there are not many who understand that this Christ-mind, or consciousness, is universal to all men, and that it is just as much yours and mine as it was that of Jesus or Buddha.

As long as you believe there is a God out there separate and apart from your being, just so long do you personalize God and set up the picture of an entity, identity, or a being outside of you. God is being, but not a being. God is being you and being me. So to set up a God separate from that Being produces the sense of separation that keeps us in ignorance. That personalizing of God, personalizing *I,* is the "veil" that brings about man's sense of separation from God. Personalizing God by accepting Jesus as the only Christ also pulls down the "veil." In fact, the personalization of Spirit is the "veil."

God Is Being

Impersonalization is the "unveiling," and the moment you know God as Being, then God is my being and God is your being. "Call no man your father upon the earth: for one is your Father, which is in heaven." Spirit is your creator and your being. This breaks down any personalization. For any group of persons to claim that they are the children of God or that they are the highest or best is personalization. There is no such thing as highest or lowest. There is no such thing as best, because all outward form that sets itself up as being spiritual is vanity. Only God is Spirit. Only *I,* the Spirit of God in you, am the son of God, and that *I* is so impersonal that unless you can look upon Jew and Gentile, Catholic and Protestant, Oriental and Occidental, white and black, and recognize that they are all of one Father, of the household of God, you cannot enter in.

When we impersonalize God and know that God is the being of Jesus Christ and that he showed this forth so that we would know that God was not only his Father but the Father of us all, then our prayers will not be a mental activity. We have tried to reach God with the mind to influence Him, "channelize" Him, whereas the mind must be still in the assurance of IS-ness: God is; I am; I and the Father are one. So we must make no mental effort to reach God, for we are already one with the Father. We must certainly not try with the mind to channel God in anyone's direction.

Was that not the sin of religion in all our wars? Were not chaplains encouraged to pray for victory for their side? What was this, if not trying to channel God? Was it not attempting to claim God for their side and exclusively for their side? But if we would be children of God, we must pray for our enemies. It does not mean that we must pray for our enemy to destroy us—not that it would make any difference if we did—but we must pray that our enemy be set free from the carnal mind just as we want our friends to be set free from the carnal mind. If, however, we set ourselves up as being God's special pets and all others as the carnal mind, we have again placed ourselves in bondage. To pray for our enemy means to know the truth about our enemy, to know that insofar as any expression of the carnal mind on the part of the enemy is concerned, it is not power, and insofar as the true identity of the enemy is concerned, it is as much God as our identity is God.

When God has been thoroughly impersonalized, the meaning of Omnipresence will be clear. We have set up a sense of separation from God even while declaring that God is omnipresence. But where am I in that Omnipresence? If God is omnipresence, then I must be that Presence, but if I am going to have a God and a "me" too, I am not impersonalizing; I am setting up a sense of separation. I have God as Omnipresence only if I am omnipresence.

I *Knocks! Do you Hear?*

"I stand at the door, and knock." In the light of what you have read so far in this book, does this not now have greater significance for you? "I stand at the door, and knock." Do you not understand that that does not mean a man who lived two thousand years ago? Do you not know that that does not mean any man today? Do you not know that that does not mean anything other than what it says, that *I* is knocking at the door and begging to be admitted, so that you will open the door of your consciousness and admit It?

I is the creative principle of this universe, and this *I* has been knocking at the door of your consciousness for centuries, begging to be admitted, and you have held It back, localizing It in the Holy Land of two thousand years ago.

The Infinite Way reveals that this very *I* is the illumined consciousness, the God-consciousness, that you are seeking. *I* is that illumination, that initiation, that enlightenment. The *I* of your being is the very food, clothing, housing, happiness, peace, and security that you are seeking. That *I* has always been knocking at the door trying to get into your consciousness.

Your entire life depends on knowing the nature of God. Until you know God aright, do not fool yourself by believing you have attained immortality, because you attain immortality only in the degree that you know Him aright. You will never know Him aright until you know Him as *I*: *I,* the Spirit of God in you; *I,* the still small voice within. The kingdom of God is within you, and God is in His kingdom. God constitutes His kingdom.

Either these words are bringing forth from within you a joyous feeling of acceptance, a feeling of "Yes, yes, I always knew that must be so," or the door of your consciousness has not opened to admit *I*, and the "veil" is still there. In that event, it will be necessary to abide in this Word and let this Word abide in you until your consciousness does open, and you do admit that *I* that is standing there knocking. What is knocking at the door is *I*. "*I* stand at the door"—not a person, but *I*, not any person, only *I*, the very *I* that is "the way, the truth, and the life," the very *I* that is the bread, the meat, the wine, and the water.

The Mystical Path Is Practical

Sometimes when a teacher or practitioner tells a student that he is keeping his health, keeping his supply and his companionship away from himself, he may ask, "How?"

Then he must be told, "You will not open the door of your consciousness and admit *Me, I*. You will not admit the *I* that is knocking there. You are looking for another God, or you are not looking for God at all, but for some fruitage, some benefit from God. This you will never find."

God does not give health; God does not give supply; God does not give peace; God does not give security. God is all of these: "I am the way, the truth, and the life. . . . I am the resurrection." The *I* does not send these or give these: the *I* is these, the *I* embodies these. When you open the door of your consciousness and admit *I*, you will find the Presence—at first slowly and gradually, because none of us could take it all in one leap—but you will find that that Presence flows out from you in the forms necessary to your daily experience.

That is why the mystical path is the most practical way of life that has ever been known. The world will try to tell us that the materialistic way is the most practical, but if you look at history I think you will agree that materialism has not given us the way. Even if you look at the countries that once had a favorable balance of trade with a steady inflow of gold, you will find how the scene has shifted and that many of them do not have it any more. Why? Because everything out in the world is as fleeting as a shadow.

But if you have opened your consciousness to *I* and have realized that *I* in the midst of you is God—that *I* in the midst of you is this Allness—then if for some reason your health, your home, or your family has left you today, it makes no difference. This *I* is the resurrection.

Once you realize that *I* in the midst of you am He, you will discover then that the lost years of the locust are restored. Everything that has ever been taken from you because of your ignorance of God is now returned to you, and twice over. None of this is possible, however, except to those who open the door of their consciousness and admit the *I* that is standing there knocking.

Pandora's Box

In the teaching of truth, you are faced with a situation comparable to Pandora's box. Pandora's box was supposed to have hidden within it a great treasure, but when it was opened, evil jumped out. So it is, too, that truth is the greatest treasure there is, but if you open the door of truth to the unprepared thought, the truth that *I* am the truth will be prostituted, because it will flap its wings and say, "I am God! I am God!" and those persons who have so little understood the truth will try to be God to you.

To persons unprepared for this truth, the revelation of *I* can be destructive because they may attempt to use it for personal gain, and also because it gives them a false sense of *I* which makes them believe that an individual has power. The truth is that no individual has power, because *I* am all-power, *I* am omnipotence. An individual has no power. You of yourself have no power. You can never direct power; you can never use power.

When you know the secret of *I,* you abide in stillness and let *I* do Its work: not you—*I,* that *I* that is in the midst of you. You need no thoughts, since you cannot and need not enlighten God. The very fact that you have reached out to an illumined consciousness is the connecting link between you and God. Then all that illumined consciousness has to do is to abide in God, and God meets your need.

The part your consciousness plays when it has been illumined is that it has awakened; it has had enough of the "unveiling" to know that the *I* of you and the *I* of anyone turning to you is God, so that there is no need to transfer thought to him, to transfer power to him, or to use God-power for him. It is the Father's good pleasure to give him the kingdom, the good pleasure of the Father, the *I* in the midst of him. *I* in the midst of you is mighty, but the *I* in the midst of you is in the midst of him because of Omnipresence. Therefore you do not have to project your thought across the miles: you only have to abide in the stillness, and because the *I* has been unveiled, the truth has been unveiled.

If you know *I,* why do you have to reach out? Is there not an *I* in you? Do you not say "I" all the time, and is not *I* God? Therefore, abide in stillness.

Understanding the nature of God as *I* is the treasure, but in revealing it, it will prove to be evil if it comes to the awareness of the unillumined, those who think that a personal sense of "I" is God, that any person can wield God-power, or that some person is specially favored by God, and therefore can do better for you than one of the other God-realized practitioners. All of this can be evil because it is personalizing. Learn to impersonalize. Only when you impersonalize can you become still inside and let *I* do the work, and not think that it is the "I" of you. Remember, there is an *I* in the person you are helping as well as in you, and It is the same *I,* the one and only *I.* Let It do the work without words and without thoughts, and then the personal sense of "I" will not get in the way.

I *Is Supply*

At one time, a student wrote me that he was having a problem of lack and asked me to do some work for supply. My answer was:

The problem really is not lack. If you will only open your eyes, you will realize that there is just as much grass on the earth as there ever was; there are just as many trees, just as much fruit, just as many cattle, just as many fish, just as many birds, just as many diamonds in the earth, just as much gold and platinum, just as many pearls in the sea. So where do you find lack?

The problem cannot be lack, because the world is full of abundance. The lack is in personalizing supply, in thinking that you do not have it. As long as you personalize in that way and set up a selfhood apart from God, you will not have supply. But when you realize that "the earth is the Lord's, and the fulness thereof" and "Son . . . all that I have is thine," you are impersonalizing.

Go up onto the mountaintop and look out on the earth as far as your eyes can see. All this, give *I* unto thee. Do you hear that word *I* again? *I.* But where have you been looking for supply? Outside? Surely you were personalizing it instead of realizing that supply is *I.* It is embodied in *I.* All that is embodied in the infinite *I* that I am and you are is yours—all the land as far as you can see. The earth and all that is therein is yours. It is *My* good pleasure to give you the Kingdom, but if you personalize, then there are those who have and those who have not.

Impersonalize yourself and see that you are not the person that you see in the mirror. That is a body, but what you are is *I.* Now you have impersonalized: you have impersonalized yourself; you have impersonalized God; and you have impersonalized supply because there is no such thing as supply that is meant merely for you or for me.

Is there a God who can give? Would that not indicate a God who is withholding? Then what kind of a God do you have? A man-made God, a God made in the image and likeness of man? Surely, a man can give and man can withhold, but can God? The moment you see that God has no power to withold the sunshine, the moon or stars, the oceans, or the fish, you know that there is no God withholding anything. You cannot really have a problem of lack. What you have is the problem of a sense of separation from God, and you in your ignorance have set up a selfhood apart from God.

In other words, you are not declaring, I am *I.* Instead, you are declaring, I am a person; and lack of education, lack of opportunity, or certain circumstances are depriving me. You are doing all this. You are making your own prison. You cannot demonstrate supply: you can only demonstrate *I.* You cannot demonstrate security; you cannot pray for security. In fact, you will never be able to save enough money to have security, as many ex-millionaires have found out. The only security you can have is when the door of your consciousness has opened and admitted the *I* so that you can say, "*I* is my supply. *I* in the midst of me is mighty."

In *The Infinite Way** it says, "That which I am seeking, I am." That sentence should be enough to save the world. But with the intellect it cannot be accepted, therefore it takes years and years of hearing it and living with it, until eventually you can say, "Yes, *I, I.* Now I understand the meaning of *I.*" You cannot personalize *I.*

In my early days in this work, when because of a problem of supply the *I* was revealed to me, that revelation ended my days of lack and limitation, but it did something more. It revealed to me that I am not man. I am *I,* and *I* am not in this body. So it is that when you are in your automobile, you are not in your automobile. You are really never a part of your automobile and you are never in it. You are always something separate and apart from it, governing it, and it is a tool that you are directing.

This same truth applies to your body. Once you realize *I,* you will know that this body has the same relationship to you that your automobile has. It is an instrument for your use, and when you are through with it, you will find yourself with a new one. But you are not in it, for *I* is Consciousness, infinite divine Consciousness, and It is omnipresent. If I and the Father are one, then I am as omnipresent as God. Otherwise there are two: one infinite and one finite. But if I and the Father are one, *I* am omnipresent.

*By the author (San Gabriel, Calif.: Willing Publishing Co., 1960), p. 107.

The Universal Nature of I *Makes Us All One*

The Infinite Way reveals the impersonal nature of God, meaning that God is not a person, that God is not localized as the mind of some one person: God is being. But God is infinite being; therefore God must be your being and my being. That is why we can accept *I* as the name of God, because I have the name of *I* and you have the name of *I.* Each one of us is *I. I* is the identity of everyone, and that is what makes us brothers and sisters. That is what makes it possible for us to meet without envy, jealousy, or malice, because no matter how much abundance this one may have or how much another may lack, it will all equalize itself as we come into the awareness of this *I.* Each one of us is *I,* and God is that infinite *I* in us.

When we have seen the universal nature of God as *I,* as the *I* of every individual and as the *I* of every cat, dog, bird, and beast, the lion and the lamb will lie down together—the human lion and lamb as well as the animal. When we recognize *I* as universal Being, infinite Being, we will make friends of our enemies—not by overcoming them, but by recognizing that *I* in the midst of the enemy am *I* in the midst of each one of us, and we are one.

There is only one *I.* The selfhood of God is the selfhood of you and the selfhood of me. If I give to you, I am giving to myself. If you give to me, you are giving to yourself. It is like transferring money from your right-hand pocket to your left. It does turn out that way, once you begin to understand the *I* which is God, knocking at the door of your consciousness.

For this reason, "Inasmuch as ye have done it unto one of the least of these my brethren, ye have done it unto me," because *I* am the least of these my brethren, and the least of these my brethren is *I.* Whatever you have done to another, you have done unto yourself, and this should help explain the meaning of karma. The evil that you do to another is bound to come back to you. There is an elastic band attached to it, and the stone you throw has to come back, but the good you do also has an elastic band, and the further and harder you throw it, the sooner it comes back to you.

The lesson we are learning is that God is individual selfhood. God is not floating around in the air any more than God is up in the sky. God is not bodiless: there cannot be a being without a body. True, the body does not have to be physical in nature, but it is a body. Every individual embodies that *I,* that divine Being. It is his individual consciousness, although It is veiled over by the belief that man is a human being, that he is mortal, that he is conceived in sin and brought forth in iniquity. It is veiled over by the belief that only a few men can know the *I,* or divine Consciousness. But God is manifest as individual you and me, and if God is to appear in the midst of us, God must appear as individual you and me.

This truth cannot be given to those who have not come to it through sufficient study and meditation, because they will turn the truth of that very *I* into something destructive to themselves, never to others. We can never really destroy others: we only destroy ourselves, and we do that through personalization, through misinterpretation.

To follow The Infinite Way, first of all, open the door of your consciousness and admit the *I* that is knocking there. Do it in secret: do not try to explain it to your friends; do not think that you are going to be able to give it to them through the human mind. They could never accept it.

To explain this great truth to those on the third-dimensional level of consciousness is not only difficult but practically impossible, and therefore you will have to feed it to them gently until they have arrived at some measure of spiritual maturity. Then you can remove that last veil without shocking them, and show them that *I* is standing at the door of their consciousness begging admittance.

CHAPTER VII

IMPERSONALIZING ERROR

There have been hundreds of mystics in the history of the world who have been lifted so high in consciousness that they have realized *I,* and yet many of them were never able to round out a happy, healthy, or successful life, nor did they ever raise up a body of students capable of revealing to the world the divine harmony that is here for everyone. Why was this? Why, when they had reached such great heights, were they still plagued with the discords of this world? The reason is that they never grasped the importance and significance of the nature of error.

Without an understanding of the nature of error, this world is not going to be any different in the next generation than it has been in this one. We all know that there have been many revelations of *I,* but we also know that these revelations have not saved the world. The revelation of the nature of error in combination with the revelation of *I,* however, can and will.

An Understanding of the Nonpower of Effect Is Essential

It is true that the nature of error was taught in some degree in the early years of metaphysical teaching and healing, but the real significance of the principle of the nothingness and nonpower of disease was not understood. It was believed that mind, which was made synonymous with God, was the power that healed the disease; in short, that God was the power that removed it. However, if you accept the truth that God is omnipotent, you most logically follow that with, "Well, then, nothing but God is power." That must mean the powerlessness of anything and everything that is appearing to you as power, whether it is person, thing, circumstance, or condition. You can then look at it objectively and realize how impossible it would be for it to be a power or have a power, if God is omnipresent and omnipotent, the only Presence and the only Power.

The more aware you become of the nature of God as Omniscience, Omnipotence, and Omnipresence, the more aware you become of the nonpower of this world of effect. You may wonder why the mystics of old did not discover this principle, and the answer is that their minds were conditioned, just as the minds of some of the mystics of today are conditioned. They believe that karma is power, more powerful even than God, or they believe that God uses evil for His purposes. They are so conditioned that they cannot surrender their belief in the power of sin, disease, false appetite, lack, and limitation. That is what makes it difficult to explain this principle to those who have not been inwardly led to such a teaching. Those of you who have been led to it can more readily accept and understand it because you probably have already experienced the nonpower of error in some form of other. Whatever you have experienced, however, is only a beginning.

The Powers of This World Are Not Power in the Presence of God

Like millions of persons today, centuries ago the Hebrews prayed to God to destroy the evils of their world, but they never were destroyed. Since the advent of Christianity, Christians have been praying to God to overcome the evils of their world, and these prayers, too, have never been successful. Persons of other religions and teachings have been praying to overcome the evils of their world, and yet they have not been overcome. And they never will be overcome until we come to the recognition that we have been wasting time fighting evil. If God could fight evil, it would not be necessary to pray to God to do it. God would be doing it without our asking Him.

Do not begin telling God about what He is not doing. God's wisdom is infinite—not your wisdom, God's. Your wisdom is infinite when you have "died" sufficiently to your beliefs, your theories, your concepts, and in meditation have opened your consciousness to receive God's wisdom. Only then is your wisdom infinite, because it is not really your wisdom but God's.

In your meditations, eventually, you will come to a deep communion with God, a tabernacling with Him. That Presence is as real and tangible as anything you have ever known, even more so; and when, through your meditations, you begin to commune with that Spirit within you, It will very quickly convince you that the powers of the world are not power, and more especially that the evil powers of the world are not evil. In fact, nothing is evil except thinking makes it so, accepting it makes it so, but in and of itself there is no evil.

In whatever measure you have experienced a spiritual healing, you have already proved this truth. In other words, if you had a cold, which is supposed to be a power, and if you have had a spiritual healing of it, then you know that what has been proved is that that cold was not the power it claimed to be.

If you have had a more serious illness, and through your own or another's spiritual consciousness you have seen the pain and the symptoms disappear and harmony restored, all that you have really experienced is the nothingness of that which had been appearing as a disease, because if it were something it would still be something. The very fact that it disappeared without material remedies, surgery, or applications of any kind means that it really was not what it claimed to be.

Evil, a Universal Hypnotism

All evil, regardless of its name or nature, is the product of a universal hypnotism or malpractice based on the belief in two powers, which Paul described as the carnal mind. Whatever discord touches us is nothing but this mesmeric sense. It is not your belief and it is not my belief: it is a universal belief which we come under by virtue of our ignorance of truth.

Through the activity of the carnal mind, operating universally, we come under this hypnotism from the moment of conception, and if we are living under the law of good and evil, anything can happen. We are subject either to the universal carnal mind, its beliefs and its activities, or we are responding more and more to the spiritual urge.

For example, in autumn with the first cold rains, probably three or four out of ten people will be sniffling, not because their wrong thinking is thus victimizing them, but because of the universal hypnotism arising out of the belief in two powers. This hypnotism we must break by realizing that we need not be subject to world mesmerism, and by understanding that hypnotism or the carnal mind is not of God, is not spiritually ordained, and has no spiritual law to uphold it. Therefore, it is not power.

We do not fight hypnotism or the carnal mind; we do not argue with it; we do not attempt to destroy it, nor to rise above it. For us, hypnotism and the carnal mind are merely names which identify good and evil as the essence of all limitation, but as we overcome the belief in the powers of good and evil, we begin to dissolve the source of our discords and inharmonies.

The more we live in the realization that we do not have to be subject to the universal hypnotism of the world belief in two powers, the more we free ourselves from that influence and live under Grace instead of under the law. When we understand God as Omnipotence, we can then realize that hypnotism, mesmerism, the universal mind, or the universal belief in two powers, is not power, and in the degree of that realization do we become free.

This universal belief of the human or carnal mind can act as power only because of our acceptance of it, but in and of itself there is no power in the suggestion of a selfhood apart from God or of a presence or power apart from God. The only presence is Omnipresence. Even though we may believe we see a ghost, even though we may see sin, disease, or death, the only presence is Omnipresence.

God is the only power, regardless of appearances, and God is omniscience, all-wisdom. Therefore, we do not have to know anything about the activity of mind or body; all we have to do is to rest in God's omniscience, rest in His infinite wisdom. As we abide in Omniscience, Omnipotence, and Omnipresence, we can state with conviction, "Ah, yes! There is no presence and there is no power other than God, and this that we call the belief in two powers—the carnal mind—this is not power. This cannot operate in or through man."

Evil Is Impersonal

All evil is impersonal: there is no person in whom, on whom, or through whom it can operate. Whether it is a claim of weather, of disease, or of lack—whatever the name or nature of the evil—it is impersonal. It does not have its rise in you, in me, or in any person, place, thing, or condition. The root of all evil is the carnal mind, or a belief in two powers; and the belief that there is power in disease, lack, or sin is the hypnotism causing all the discord in the world.

To the degree we realize that in all this world there exists no such thing as good or evil as an entity are we without a carnal mind. Therefore, even to think or say that some thing, person, or condition is *good* is to permit the carnal mind to control us. There is only one Being, one Essence, one Power, and that is Consciousness—God. Consciousness is neither good nor evil: It just *IS*.

For Consciousness to be good or evil, It would have to have an opposite and It would have to have degrees. There are no opposites in God; there are no degrees in God: God is infinite; God is omnipresent, omnipotent, omniscient, and that leaves no room for opposites, for opposition, limitation, or finiteness. As we permit limitation and finiteness to operate in our consciousness, we bring the carnal mind into our experience. The carnal mind is not overcome by fighting it, but by recognizing that it is made up of the belief in good and evil.

We Recognize Good and Evil in Human Experience

This does not mean that in our everyday human experience we do not take cognizance of good and evil. Naturally, we recognize that a condition of health is a better expression in our experience than one of disease, and one of the fruits of spiritual living is a greater sense of health than we may now be enjoying. So while it is true that humanly we seem compelled to acknowledge the limitations of good and evil, we must recognize that Consciousness does not embody within Itself quantities or qualities of good or evil, or of limitation.

As we engage in the routine activities of the day, we inwardly maintain our spiritual awareness of the *I* as individual consciousness and acknowledge that whatever appears in our experience as sin, disease, death, or limitation is the carnal mind, the "arm of flesh," or no mind.

We do not deny that there are poor drivers on the road, drunken drivers, incompetent and even reckless drivers. As far as the human picture is concerned, the highways are filled with both good and evil persons, but having recognized that, we take our spiritual stand: "Yes, that is the appearance due to the belief in good and evil—carnal mind—but it is not power: it is not God-ordained, God-maintained, or God-sustained. It is but the 'arm of flesh.' "

Throughout our human experience, we cannot avoid being aware of the sin, disease, and poverty in the world, conditions that will be in the world as long as there is a human race that has not become emancipated. As long as there is a world made up of the belief in good and evil, these pictures will always be here for us to see: sickness all around, death, insanity, and all those things that go to make up the carnal mind. What determines the harmony of our experience is our reaction to these—not hiding our heads in the sand and claiming or declaring that they do not exist, but recognizing, "Yes, they are the 'arm of flesh.' They do have temporal power. They are power to a world that believes in good and evil, but not to me. I know that there is but one Power."

At the beginning of our spiritual journey, we are merely coming out of the mortal sense of evil into a better sense of human life, one that is healthier, wealthier, or happier. But that is not the ultimate of life. The ultimate of life is spiritual realization which eventually takes us out of both the evil and the good sense of human life.

The Omnipotence of I

As you witness the evils of this world, as they turn up in your experience, your family's, your neighbor's, or your nation's, be sure in your meditation that you cover the two major principles of The Infinite Way: first, open the door of your consciousness and admit the *I,* and acknowledge:

> *Be not afraid,* I *am with you. Be not afraid of those out there:* I *am He.* I *am here, and* I *am there. Be not afraid:* I *in the midst of you am mighty.* I *am life eternal.* I *am the way. Just rely on* Me. *Fear no danger, for there*

is no power external to you. I *in the midst of you am infinite power, the all-power, the only power.*

Live by Grace, since I *am your meat, your wine, your water.* I *can give you water, and if you drink of it you will never thirst again.* I *have meat the world knows not of.* I *am the resurrection.* I *am the way:* I *am the way to your peace;* I *am the way to your abundance;* I *am the way to your safety.*

I *am the rock.* I *am a fortress.* I *am a high tower. Abide in* Me *and let* Me *abide in you, and no evil shall come nigh thy dwelling place. No weapons that are formed against thee shall prosper. Why? They are shadows; they are not realities; they are not powers.* I *in the midst of you am omnipotence, the only power. These arrows, these poisoned darts, these germs, these bullets, these bombs: they are shadows. They are beliefs in a power apart from* Me. *They are a universal belief in two powers. Believe in* Me *as Omnipotence.*

You are never in mysticism until you have opened your consciousness and accepted the truth that *I* in the midst of you am He, that Christ was incarnated in you, and that the Annunciation means the conception of the Christ in you. Your recognition of this truth is the birth of the Christ in you. But, when you accept this, do not forget that it is not complete until you have followed up the omnipotence of *I*, which is the first principle of The Infinite Way, with the second, which is the nonpower of that which is appearing as the world of effect.

Recognize Evil As the Carnal Mind

In your experience you will be dealing with persons of different states of consciousness, of varying degrees of good and of evil, and even if they do not touch you personally, you will be cognizant of evil in persons active in national or international affairs. It is not enough, I can assure you, to bear witness to the fact that the Christ is in them. You must take the second step as well and recognize that the carnal mind is not power. Only this completes your prayer or your meditation. Until you have acknowledged, "*I* in the midst of me is God; *I* in the midst of you is God; and the carnal mind, the universal belief in two powers, is nonpower," then, and then alone, have you completed it.

Do not try to destroy evil in a person. Realize the universal nature of the carnal mind, and then "nothingize" it. This can be done because God never created a carnal mind. God never created two powers. God never created evil, and therefore, as you impersonalize and "nothingize," you bring your prayer, treatment, or realization to a conclusion. Then you can rest and be certain that you have really handled the situation intelligently and spiritually because you have done honor to God in acknowledging Omnipotence. You have done honor to God in acknowledging Omnipresence, the presence of God within you, the very *I* of your being, and you have thereby practically wiped out the devil in the realization that the carnal mind, the universal belief in two powers, has no law of God to maintain it.

The evil that comes nigh your dwelling place always personalizes itself. It comes as a sin, as a temptation, or as a false appetite in you or in some other person. It always personalizes itself in "him," "her," or "you." Watch it, and you will notice that you never think about alcoholism: you just think about the alcoholic. You never think about drug addiction: you think about the drug addict. You never think about the universal carnal mind: you think about the evil man in prison, because evil always comes in a personalized form. It came to Jesus in the form of a devil. It always personalizes itself, but when Jesus turned on the devil, there was no devil there. It was just a temptation in his mind, and it had to be met in his mind.

So, there is no evil person confronting you. There is no evil condition confronting you. This is a personalization of the impersonal carnal mind—not your belief or mine, but the universal belief in two powers. As you recognize this and impersonalize it, the evil falls away from the person, whether it is a sin, disease, false appetite, or whatever it may be. It falls away from him sometimes very quickly and sometimes slowly, depending upon his degree of receptivity.

No God-Power Is Used

When you learn to impersonalize evil, you do not have to call upon a God-power. You can accept God as Omnipotence, but only if you can see so-called evil appearances as *maya* or illusion, and thus not try to get God to do something to them. When you can do this, you are in spiritual wisdom. Then you can say to the blind man, "Open thine eyes." The moment you try to get a God-power to do something for the blind, however, you have lost the demonstration.

If you can look at the impotent man and say, "Rise, take up thy bed, and walk," you can help him, but when you turn to God to do something for him you are in the same dream that he is in. The spiritually illumined know that there is no need to call on God for anything because God is always about His business. He does not have to be reminded, directed, or pleaded with.

If you really want to honor God, know that God is always being God; God is always maintaining and sustaining His spiritual universe. Then, in your release of God, you realize, "What power is there apart from God? What presence is there apart from God? I must not be deceived by appearances." Then you see rightness reveal itself. No God-power is used. God-power was there in the beginning, but the recognition of Omnipotence and Omniscience and the unreal nature of appearances brings it into infinite manifestation.

Awake Out of Inertia into Being

It is in our lap! It is within our power to determine whether or not we value our freedom enough to break through the mental inertia that would keep us from consciously realizing truth two, three, or more times a day.

Every one of us has a spiritual destiny. Then, what keeps us from experiencing it? The belief in two powers, good and evil, which has become so crystallized in human consciousness as to form a malpractice, or hypnotism, that keeps us under the law instead of under Grace! Once we know the truth that every form of discord in our life is a form of hypnotism, and to the extent that we can accept God-being, we release ourselves from the sins, the fears, and the diseases of this world. Our mind is not then reaching out to God, nor is it seeking good: we are completely released from seeking anything. God is, *I* am; and we rest in that.

My life and God's life are joined: it is the one life. My mind and God's mind are the one mind. Nothing can separate us or divide us. Not even life or death can separate me from the life of God, the love of God, and the abundance of God, for God is being now. *I cannot make it so—not even God can make it so: it has been so from the beginning.*

What God has joined together no man, no circumstance, and no condition can put asunder, and any belief that I have heretofore accepted of a presence or a power apart from the I *that I am, I consciously reject because of Omnipotence and Omnipresence.*

Impersonalize God; impersonalize evil. Know the nature of *I* as universal being, universal life. Do not allow the "veil" that personalizes God to be put back on. Make no image of God: do not make a wood carving; do not make an ivory carving or a gold carving; do not make even a mental image of God. Then you will not be personalizing God.

The minute you have an image of God in your thought, you are personalizing, and you are expecting that concept to be God, and a concept cannot be God. Only *I* can be God, and you cannot have a mental image of *I*. That is the one word that defies description. Try as you will, you cannot make a mental image of *I*.

Once this truth has been unveiled for you, it will never be veiled for you again. You will never be able to go back to making concepts of God or looking for God to do something to the nothingness and nonpower of this world of effect. Always that smile will come to your lips, and the word *I* will come, and you will be at peace, you will be at rest. Then, in quietness and confidence, you can be a beholder of God in action. You do not impel It; you do not empower It; you do not send It forth: in quietness and confidence, you become a beholder watching It at work.

CHAPTER VIII

I SPEAKS

Within each one of us there is a Presence, a Something more real than anything we can know, with a vision beyond our vision. This it is that is living our life for us. Too often, however, because we are not aware of this Presence, we are determined to live our own life: to make our own decisions and to rely on our personal wisdom, judgment, or strength; but that is only because we have not yet come into the actual experience of This that is within us.

Before this Presence makes Itself known to us, there usually comes a period in which we recognize that It exists. On the metaphysical and sometimes on the spiritual path, the student can believe this only because it is told to him by a teacher who has experienced It or because in the scriptural writings of the world he has read that It exists.

In one way or another, regardless of how It is brought to our attention, there must come an awareness that there is a Presence within, a He that is greater than he that is in the world, a Spirit. With this knowledge comes the continuous recognition that It abides within us, that It walks beside us, that It is our vision, our guidance, and our direction. There must be an abiding in that truth until the Experience comes to our conscious awareness. When It does, It speaks very much as we might imagine the Master speaking: "Fear not, *I* am with you. *I* will never leave you nor forsake you. *I* will be with you to the end of the world." It often speaks in the word *I*: "It is *I*; be not afraid," and It continually brings to our awareness the fact that we are not walking the earth alone.

The Tree Includes Its Branches

Sometimes we feel that when we acknowledge God in us, or the Christ indwelling, we are indulging duality or twoness, but this is not true. It cannot be explained logically any more than God can be explained, but the truth is that this *I* within us, this presence of God, does not make for duality because It is actually the Self of our being —not only the Self of my being but also the Self of your being.

This Self and you are one, but It is greater than you. Can you not see that what is invisible, the Source of your inspiration, the Source of your life, the Cause and the creative Principle of your life, even though you are one with It, is greater than you? It is greater in the same sense that we speak of the branch of a tree and the tree as if they were two, but a branch of a tree and a tree are not two: they are one, one tree, and the tree includes the branch.

So God includes individual being, just as the whole tree includes the branches. There is no such thing as the life of a tree and the life of a branch of the tree. The life of the tree is the life of the branch as long as they are one, but from the moment the branch is severed from the tree that life withers.

So the human being who sees himself separate and apart from God is withering, going toward his threescore years and ten, a few years less or a few years more. But everyone must learn that there are adjustments that take place in the life of every individual as this thing called time goes on. He must realize that he will not always have his friends, relatives, parents, or children, because in the human scheme of life, where the human being lives as a branch separate from the tree, there is birth and there is death, and the very birth itself is the forerunner of the death that is to come.

There is only one way in which this can be overcome, and that is to realize that since we are a branch of the Tree, one with the Tree, we have no branch-life, no life that has a beginning, no life that has an ending. We have the infinite and eternal life of the whole Tree. Because of our relationship to the Tree, a branch that is one with the Tree, we have no personal responsibility, no personal life. We have the Life which is God. A branch could say, "I and the tree are one, but the tree is greater than I." So can we say, "I am one with the Life which is God, yet the Life which is God is greater than any of Its branches. It is even greater than the sum total of all Its branches."

Reestablishing Our Unity with the Tree of Life

To bring this relationship into active expression in our lives, there must be a specific act. When the Prodigal realized his situation as separate and apart from his father, when he realized to what a state his desire to be something of himself had brought him, he got up and started the journey back to his father's house. He did not continue sitting there; he got up and started back.

There comes a moment in our lives when we realize that we have lived as human beings cut off from our Source. We have been the branch separate and apart from the Tree of Life. When we realize that, we perform an act. This act is described in Scripture as "repent, and turn yourselves." It is an act in which we consciously make an about-face and declare:

I have been living separate and apart from God; I have been living the life of a human being, living by bread, water, and air; I have been living by external means. Now I return to the Father's house, and I realize consciously that from now on I am fed from the eternal Spring that is within me. I am fed by the bread of Life, the staff of Life which I *am. I draw from within, from my Father's storehouse.*

Recognize Me

As we abide in this truth, there comes an experience. It may come with an assurance from within:

I *have never left you.* I *have never been separate or apart from you.* I *have walked with you every step of the way, awaiting your recognition. Long have* I *awaited you; long have* I *awaited your awakening; long have* I *awaited your return; long have* I *awaited your recognition. Look within, and find* Me, *for* I *am within you.* I *am the very fabric, the very source of your life.*

The headaches you have known, the problems you have suffered—all these have been only because of this sense of separation which has kept your gaze on the outer realm, instead of compelling you to turn it within where I *am to be found.* I *am to be found within your consciousness, within your awareness.* I *am to be found in quietness, in stillness, in confidence.*

Be not afraid; be not afraid, it is I. I, *the* I *that is speaking to you, is the* I *of that army that is marching against you. The* I *that is your abiding place, your dwelling place, is the* I *of the being of your friends and of your foes.* I *dwell in you, and* I *dwell in them. As* I *dwell in you, so do* I *dwell in them and so do* I *dwell in all. In meeting friend and in meeting foe, you are meeting* Me. *Recognize* Me *in the midst of you. Then recognize* Me *in the midst of your friends, and recognize* Me *in the midst of your foes.*

Recognize that there is but one divine Selfhood, one Father of all, and you will soon see that the only enemies you ever had consisted of your own belief in a selfhood separate and apart from Me. *Even if you recognize* Me *as your selfhood, you may still have thought of others as having some selfhood apart from* Me. *But* I *am your selfhood, and* I *am the selfhood of all those others.*

I *am your staff of life;* I *am your wisdom;* I *am your bread, your meat, your wine, and your water; but* I *am this to all men.* I *am this in the midst of your friends and your loved ones, and* I *am this in the midst of your foes.*

Recognize Me *in the midst of all, and then you will find that* I *am in all, and* I *greet you through all.* I *greet you through those you thought were your friends, and* I *greet you through those you thought were your enemies; for you can never be greeted by any other than* I *because* I *am infinite.* I *am infinite omnipresence;* I *am omnipotent omnipresence;* I *am the presence that stands within you, before you, beside you, behind you.* I *am that presence; therefore be not afraid, it is* I. *It is* I.

I *am not in the whirlwind, and therefore recognize that there is no power in a whirlwind. The only power there is, is in* I, *that* I AM THAT I AM *which is the life of your being, the life of your friend's being, the life of your enemy's being.* I *am the life of all being.*

The Universality and Omnipresence of the Presence

When this Presence announces Itself to you in an inner assurance that It is present, remember that this means not only Its presence in you, but Its infinite omnipresence. It is not announcing that God is present in you, separate and apart from all others. It is announcing that this *I* is present in you, present in me, present in him, present in her, present in it. In other words, you cannot "finitize" God; you cannot channel God to be in one person or in one place. When you recognize the presence of God, you are recognizing the universal presence of God.

When, before you enter your automobile, you are given the assurance from within, "*I* am with you, and *I* go with you," remember that this does not mean you, separate and apart from everyone else on the road. It means you are to recognize "*My* presence," the divine Presence, as being Omnipresence, All-presence, Everywhere-presence, and in any particular moment you can realize that Presence.

So it is that when the Spirit is announcing Itself and Its presence, It is not saying to me, "Joel, *I* am present in you." No, It is saying,

"*I* am present." How tragic it would be if God could announce, "*I* am present with you, Joel," and then leave out everybody else. Such a thing is not possible. When the Father assures you, "*I* am present with thee; *I* go with thee wherever thou goest; *I* will never leave thee," God is announcing His presence equally everywhere, universally. He is announcing Omnipresence: the Presence in you, the Presence in those near and those far because there are none near or far. All this universe and all its people are embraced in your consciousness.

My consciousness is infinite, and I embrace in my consciousness the Jews and the Gentiles, the Occidentals and the Orientals, the Africans, the Asians, and persons of all types and places and kinds. I embrace in my consciousness Americans, Canadians, Russians, French, and English. I embrace in my consciousness this entire universe because my consciousness is infinite.

I can close my eyes and instantaneously have within me the peoples of all races and of all ages: past, present, and future. My consciousness is large enough to embody all of these, and therefore, if the presence of God is with me in my consciousness, then the presence of God is with everyone and everything in my consciousness, and nothing exists outside of my consciousness, for my consciousness is infinite. Why is it infinite? Because God and I are one, and all that the Father has is mine. Therefore all the God-consciousness is my consciousness individualized, and that Consciousness embraces all there is in this universe that constitutes the world, and the worlds beyond worlds, and the worlds of outer space.

If these were not embodied in our consciousness, we could have no knowledge of them; but because they are embodied in our consciousness, we will eventually know all about them, just as we are discovering the secrets of outer space. Why are we now attaining the secrets of outer space? Because these secrets are not in outer space. They are embodied in our consciousness, and we are discovering them there; they are being revealed to us there. Every person who is working with problems of outer space is working with something that is within range of his own consciousness, or he could not be aware of it. Therefore outer space is in our consciousness, and be assured God also is there.

There may be no church in outer space. I would not know. But God is in outer space. There is no place where life is not, no place where the Spirit is not. Why? Because all that exists, exists in Consciousness, and that Consciousness is mine and that Consciousness is yours. The Master said it in these words: "Thou, Father, art in me, and I in thee." We are all embodied in the divine Consciousness which is God. Our awakening to this truth brings it into conscious experience.

The Holy Ground of I

I am with you means that *I* am with all. But a thousand will still fall at your left and at my left, and ten thousand at our right until they awaken to the presence of *Me,* the presence that *I AM*, the Presence that is within them. As each individual awakens to that Presence, that individual in some measure becomes free, free of the limitations of mortal sense, free of the limitations that would set one person apart from another, or one person's interests apart from another.

I *in the midst of you am where you are.* I *in the midst of you am where your friends are.* I *in the midst of you am where your enemies are.*

There is no place, no time, no space, no person where I *am not. Be not afraid; it is* I*—whether you are looking into the face of your friend or the face of your foe, whether you are looking into the face of a placid lake or of a raging storm. Be not afraid; it is* I. *Omnipresence! Omnipresence! There is no power in the whirlwind; there is no power in the storm; there is no power in the problem.* I *am there;* I *am the only power. Besides* Me, *there are no powers, and* I *am omnipresence.*

"In my Father's house are many mansions: if it were not so, I would have told you. I go to prepare a place for you." Always remember that in My *house, in this divine Consciousness, there are many mansions. Remember that*

I *in the midst of you go to prepare a place for you. Whether you remain at home or leave home for business, marketing, or shopping,* I *am there to prepare a place for you.*

You bring this *I* into tangible expression only in the degree of your conscious awareness of It. There must be action; there must be conscious action, conscious recognition. "Repent. . . . Turn yourselves, and live ye. . . . In all thy ways acknowledge him, and he shall direct thy paths. . . . Thou wilt keep him in perfect peace, whose mind is stayed on thee."

Action! Action! Action! An activity of consciousness! And as your consciousness is active in truth, with truth, through truth, you will find that the truth, active in your consciousness, becomes the very fabric of the new life.

Not Yesterday, Not Tomorrow: Only Today

You must learn to live as if there were no yesterdays, as if there had been no mistakes yesterday and no sins yesterday. You have to live as if yesterday had passed. Just as you mark off the date on your calendar or pull off the sheet of the month gone by and throw it into the wastebasket, so do you have to tear up your entire past consciously and actively and live as if today were the only day given you to live. If you try to relive yesterday, you will be reliving its mistakes and errors, so you might as well make up your mind to let bygones be bygones.

Let yesterday go, and live as if this were the day the Lord had made, and no other. Only this day is made, not yesterday and not tomorrow. Yesterday is not made, and tomorrow is not made. Our mistakes are over and done with; our sins are over and done with; our fears are over and done with. Now, now is the appointed day.

Now is the day in which I recognize the Spirit of God present within me, and thereby recognize the presence of God present within you: you, my friends, and you, my enemies, those who like me and those who do not. I recognize

God in the midst of all. I greet the God in them, and they in turn recognize the God in me. There are no yesterdays; all this is happening today.

When midnight comes and goes, it is still today—still today in which I am living in the life of Omnipresence, still today in which I am living in the realization of a Presence within me that goes before me to prepare mansions, that goes to prepare a place for me. Now! Today! Today!

Without meditation, such an unfoldment as this cannot come. It cannot come from the air; it cannot come from outside; it has to come from within. But if it is to come from within, how can it come if there are not periods of quiet, of rest, of confidence, of assurance, periods of listening to this *I* that is in the midst of us? How can we be taught of the Spirit if we do not sit down to commune with that Spirit, and let It reveal Itself to us in wisdom, in truth, in life, in love?

The Activity of Meditation Within Changes the Without

Meditation is an activity. It is not a laziness, either physical or mental, even though others looking at us in meditation may think that we are trying to escape from the world. We are not trying to escape from the world: we are trying to meet the reality of the world which is within us. Outside of us, the picture is always changing in accord with the changing of our consciousness, but the world outside will never change for the better if there is not something from inside to bring it about, and that something is this recognition:

There is a Presence, and this Presence is within me to instruct me and to give me light. Just as the life of the tree is flowing up through the trunk and out into the branches, so is the Life which is God flowing universally in the invisible, and yet I can feel It pouring into me, the branch, individually. As It pours into me as a branch, so too It is pouring Itself into all those out in the world who are also branches, giving them newness of life, which in time will appear as leaves, buds, blossoms, and finally fruitage, rich fruitage.

A branch cannot bear fruit of itself. A branch can bear fruit only by virtue of its oneness with its source. I of my own self can do nothing; but by my turning within, the Father instructs, feeds, guides, directs, and protects me, goes before me, walks beside me and behind me, above and beneath, for this I *that is within me is omnipresence. It rides the planes; It rides the submarines; It rides the ships, the trains, the automobiles. It is omnipresence; It is omnipresence within me and within you, wherever I may be and wherever you may be.* I *in the midst of me am the life of all being.* I *in the midst of me am the safety, the security, the peace, the prosperity, and the joy of all being.*

My joy no man takes from me. Why? Because my joy is not dependent on baubles outside in the world; my joy is not due to the fruit on my tree: my joy is mine because of the omnipresence of Life which inevitably must appear as fruit. I glory not in the fruit on my tree, but in the Spirit of God in me which is the fabric of the fruit which is to appear. I can take the fruit, eat it, sell it, or use it; but within me is the Substance, the Essence, the I, *the Presence, the Fabric of all the fruit that is to come for every today that there is unto eternity.*

I glory not in outer prosperity or outer health; I glory in the Essence which fills me, this divine Presence, so that I can spend what I have today and be renewed. I can give and I can share all that the Father gives me, and yet retain within myself the Presence, the Substance, the Staff of life which, in Its season, appears outwardly as still another message, still another dollar, still another trip, still another healing, still another something or other. Always within me is the Essence, the Substance, the Fiber, the Fabric of that which is to appear externally.

Our conscious recognition of this truth is what makes available to us the presence of the Spirit of God within us.

Turn from the Problem to I

Whenever a problem arises in your experience or the experience of others who turn to you for help, do not try to search in your mind for a solution to the problem, because then you are looking for a human solution or a human working out of the problem. Instantly turn away from the problem in the realization that this *I* within is Spirit, and it is this Spirit that is the solution to all problems.

Wait in your meditation until you have the feeling of this Presence, and then release the problem to It, and let it go. Do not dwell on the problem. Instead, see in what way *I*, the Spirit within you, will solve the problem. *I* will go out and do whatever work is necessary for you to do, work which you could not outline, which you could never conceive of, and which you could never believe. You could not do it, and you could never give any advice that would bring it about. All you can do is turn from it in the realization that *I* within you is the solution of the problem, and then wait in your meditation until you do feel that Presence. When you do, loose the problem and let it go. Do not let the problem come back into your mind. Keep it out of your mind, for you have released it unto the *I* that you are, the *I* that is within you. Then, a day, two, or three days later, you will watch how It has solved the problem in a way you could never have understood or accomplished.

Two or More Gathered Together

"Where two or three are gathered together in my name, there am I in the midst of them," where two or more are gathered in the recognition of this *I* as Omnipresence. When we meet together and we are in the conscious remembrance that *I AM* in the midst of me, meaning *I AM* in the midst of you, and that *I AM* in the midst of all the others, then we are the two or more gathered in the name *I*, the name that I am.

It would make no difference where we were, in an Infinite Way class, at a supper, or a picnic. If we were consciously aware that the presence of *I* in us is the presence of *I* in everyone, we would be the two or more gathered together in that Name, as long as we continued to abide in that realization.

You can see the miracle and the magic of this. I cannot be envious of the *I* that I am, even if the *I* that I am is you. I cannot steal or want to steal from myself, and so, when I recognize that my Self is you, I cannot take anything from you. In this recognition we share with one another. Why? Because it is the Self sharing with the Self, two or more gathered together in the one name *I, I* in the midst of us.

There could be no fighting at any level, no discord or inharmony, if there were the constant recognition of *I.* It is *I* here; it is *I* there; and it is the same *I,* for we are one.

Release! Release! Release!

Once a day, in your meditations, remember consciously to release God in the sense of releasing Him from any responsibility for the evils of the world, whether they are the evils that have come nigh your dwelling place or anyone else's, or the collective evils of this world. Remember to release God in the sense of realizing consciously that no evil has its source in God, and that nothing that does not emanate from God has power.

In that same meditation, also release all mankind from the penalty of their sins. "Father, forgive them; for they know not what they do." They may be the sins of friends or the sins of foes; they may be the sins of your nation or the sins of other nations. But always remember that there must be a release, and it must be a conscious activity within you.

Father, forgive them; for they know not what they do. Forgive them as I would be forgiven. Whatever error still lurks in me, Father, forgive me, for I do not do it consciously or willfully.

In this way, then, in releasing God from the responsibility for the evils of the world, we take all power out of the erroneous or evil nature of the world, because the major power it has comes from a universal belief that God is the cause of the world's discords and woes. Therefore, when we release God from that, it is as if we were releasing the power of evil itself into nothingness.

In the same way, as we release every individual, we are fulfilling the Lord's Prayer. "Forgive us our debts, as we forgive our debtors." Forgive us in proportion as we forgive those who trespass against us. There must be a conscious release every day. I do not care whether we are talking of Americans or Russians, of the government of the United States or of Russia. I do not care whether we are talking of Chinese, Spanish, or whatnot: "Father, forgive them; for they know not what they do."

Then you will find the release that you bring about within yourself. It is said that what we loose is loosed with us, and what we bind is bound with us. So it is that within ourselves, as we release God from responsibility, we find that we have released ourselves from these ills. As we release sinners from the responsibility for their sins, the sinners that we ourselves are, are released from our sins of omission and commission. In our human experience, it is impossible not to sin. We are sinning every day in bearing false witness against somebody or other, and this we do, whether it is friend or foe. We bear false witness every day. In many ways, we fall far short of that mark which is Christhood. But we are not forgiven our sins except as we forgive those who sin against us or against this world.

Above all, be not afraid. Be not afraid, for it is I. *In quietness and in confidence, shalt thou realize that* I *in the midst of thee am mighty. In quietness and in confidence, thou shalt realize, "Be not afraid. They have only the 'arm of flesh,' carnal weapons."* I *in the midst of thee am mighty, and* I *will never leave thee, nor forsake thee. Only be not afraid, be not afraid!*

CHAPTER IX

THE TEMPLE NOT MADE WITH HANDS

There is within every person the Christ-Self, the real Self, the *I*. On the spiritual path, the goal is the attaining of conscious union with that Self, or the attaining of the realization of the Christ as our identity. This requires a "dying daily" to the human part of us, the outer part, and being reborn as this true identity; "dying" to the limited sense of self and being reborn into or as our perfected Self, the Christ-Self.

On the other hand, if we can overcome the human self, if we can "die," if we can put off that human self with its belief in good and evil and awaken to our true identity, then we are through with patchwork, through with demonstrating some good today and wondering what we will have to meet next year.

Within each of us is the perfect Self that has never fallen, has never left heaven, and therefore can never gain heaven. It is already a state of heaven; it is already living the perfected life, the spiritual life, the Christ-life that can never be crucified, can never be resurrected, cannot ever be ascended. It already is the perfect Self, the son of God, or the Christ within us. It has been called "the hidden manna," the "pearl of great price," the robe of immortality.

That son of God is you; it is I. Actually, it is our Self, and we do not patch It up; we do not demonstrate for It; we do not heal It; we cannot even make progress with It. We can, however, bring to light in our experience this perfected Self, our Christ-Self. But in order to accomplish this we do not go into meditation with the idea of meeting an outside problem, for our spiritual goal is not developing a self that has no problems, but "dying" to the self that has them or does not have them, and being reborn to our already perfected Self.

To Give Spiritual Help, Reject All Concepts

When we go into meditation, we cannot take into it any thought about the problem. This applies to any situation or person. For example, if we have children or grandchildren and want to be of any help to them, not through outwardly teaching them anything but through our inner realization, let us realize now that we have to dismiss them from thought. We do not take them into thought as if we would improve them, as if we would help them, but now in this minute, as we sit here, we are to realize:

There is no individual such as I am seeing in my mind's eye; there is no such self; there is no such person, because he about whom I am thinking is not the image and likeness of God. That is not God-created. That is the false sense of self I am entertaining about this child.

The real truth is that God created this child in His own image and likeness as pure spiritual Being, the very manifestation of God's own being expressed as this child, immortality's own being expressed as this individual being, God's selfhood revealed as this individual, not created but revealed, God's selfhood embodying only the qualities of God, embodying all the quantities of God.

"Son, . . . all that I have is thine," not a little bit of it. God cannot be

divided and a tiny bit of It put in this child. All the nature of God is expressed as this individual. All the nature of God, all the spiritual nature, all the incorporeal nature, all the eternal and immortal nature of God is now appearing.

My function, then, is to get acquainted with this child as he really is, not to continue seeing him as a human identity. Let me forget the picture I have drawn of this child and let me get acquainted with him. Let me commune with this offspring of God and come to know him.

I reject all my former concepts of this child. I have no interest in the world's opinion of him or even in his own opinion of himself. What I am seeking now is that God reveal to me the name and the nature of this child, reveal to me the true identity of this child.

Lifting Up the Son of God

You will notice that we have taken none of the child's problems into our thought. We have no thought of the child's body or of the child's mind. All that we are tabernacling with is the image and likeness of God, the child that is manifesting the spiritual nature of God in all God's completeness. We do not know what that spiritual offspring is or what it is like, but in our meditation we are asking God to reveal his name and nature to us, his identity.

I am not dealing with a good-natured child or a bad-natured child; I am not communing with an intelligent child or a not-so-intelligent child: I am communing now with God's child, the holy one of Israel, the perfected one, the Christ of God, God's spiritual offspring.

Your body is not a physical one. Know ye not that your body is the temple of God, and God is in that temple, spiritual, harmonious, whole? You are the perfected one of Israel, the perfected one of the household of God. This is the One I am knowing; this is the One with whom I am communing.

The land you are to inhabit is not a physical country with a flag. Yours is the kingdom of God. Yours is the spiritual kingdom which is peopled with God's own being infinitely manifested, God's life infinitely lived.

Your household is not one of human parents, brothers, and sisters. Your household is the household of God, the temple of God.

Our meditation can be for a husband or wife, a mother or father, a sister or brother, or for our neighbor: our neighbor next door or our neighbor across the ocean. We can begin with all our friendly neighbors, and then we can go on to our enemy neighbors. But in each case we are not going into meditation to change humanhood from evil to good, from sick to well, or from poor to rich. In each case we are meditating so as to get acquainted with our neighbor, the neighbor we are supposed to love and whom, in the human picture, we find it sometimes impossible to love.

In my true identity, I am that Christ, that perfected one that you are. But if I look at myself as I appear to be, I know how far short I fall. Regardless of where I am on the spiritual path, I am very, very far short of my Christhood, and this I know better than anyone else. If you do not know that about yourself, it is time to wake up and realize that your humanhood is no more the manifestation and completeness of what you really are spiritually than night is like day. As a matter of fact, you do not even know the nature of your true Being. The only guide you have is good humanhood, and that is not enough, because not all of the very best humanhood possible has even a trace of the spiritual in it.

Go Beyond the Demonstration of Good Humanhood

You have to go beyond humanhood; you have to go beyond the best humanhood that has ever been known before you can find spiritual identity. You have to be able to blot out of your thought your most loving qualities, most generous qualities, friendliest qualities. All these must go in order that you can say, "Ah, yes, but what is spiritual identity like? What is spiritual Selfhood like? I am trying to discover what the Master meant when he said, 'My peace I give unto you.' What kind of peace does our spiritual identity give? What kind of peace is that?"

You must think beyond the demonstration of healthy humanhood, wealthy humanhood, and happy humanhood. You must pierce the veil of illusion that separates you from the realization of your immortal Self, your Christ-Self, your real identity, the perfected Self which you are, which has no qualities of good humanhood or bad humanhood.

Again we come to that word "I" and the two ways of using it. There is the "I" that refers to our humanhood. That is the "I" that has problems and is always overcoming something. But there is that other *I* which has never had a problem, which was never born and which will never die. It is the *I* that I am, the *I* that constitutes our spiritual identity, that is under the law of God. It is the *I* that we spiritually are which lives by Grace, and whether we are thinking of our children, of a patient, a student, or a member of our family, that is the *I* with which we are tabernacling and communing. We are not communing with the humanhood of these persons. We have no interest in it, good or bad. We are seeking to enter into a spiritual communion with the Christ of them, with their perfected Self, that which is hidden behind their external appearance.

Let "I" "Die" That I *May Be Revealed*

If I go into meditation thinking of myself or of a human being whom I would like to heal, enrich, or make happy, then I am back in the metaphysical world, and probably even in the psychological or psychiatric world that has as its goal improving a human being, which improvement usually is not permanent. But if I am on the spiritual path, I go within and drop that human self, that human sense of "I," and refuse to make any attempt to improve it, heal it, correct it, purify it, or enrich it. I ignore the appearances and abide in this *I:*

The I *that I am has spiritual dominion. The* I *that I am lives by Grace and is endowed with the grace of God.*

I *already have meat;* I *already have the allness of spiritual harmony, spiritual Grace, spiritual life, and spiritual love.* I *already am the meat, the wine, and the water.*

I *already am the resurrection:* I *am the ascended one;* I *am the perfected one. By virtue of my oneness with the Father,* I *already am clothed with immortality;* I *already am eternal being. My oneness, that original relationship given me in the beginning, this establishes me in heaven.*

This I *was never born and has no need to count birth dates. This* I *will never die and does not have to concern Itself with the future. It already has an immortal and an eternal existence, and it makes no difference whether it is lived in England, the United States, Africa, or what is called this side or the other side. The* I *that I am is still the* I. *It looked out through my eyes at one year of age; It looked out through my eyes at thirty years; It is looking out through my eyes now; and I can assure you that the* I *that I am will be living, looking out and being a thousand years from now and a million years from now, because* I *and the Father are one, not two.*

All the immortality that the Father is, I *am; all the eternality that the Father is,* I *am; all the spirituality that the Father is, all of the invisibility that the Father is,* I *am.* I *am already the resurrected one.*

Throughout this meditation, I have let that other "I" with its problems die, drop out of my consciousness, and if I persist in this, one day it will not come back again, it will not intrude into my mind. This may help you understand the Master when he speaks out from the *I.* Probably it was in the early part of his ministry that he said, "I can of mine own self do nothing. . . . If I bear witness of myself, my witness is not true." But now you can understand far better how it is that later he was able to say, "He that hath seen me hath seen the Father. . . . I and my Father are one."

You will now see him ascended before the Crucifixion, ascended in consciousness to the realization of his true identity. Now he is looking out from up there, not a man with problems, not a man with a future, not a man with a mission. Now he is just the image and likeness of God, saying, "Thou seest me, thou seest the Father, for I and the Father are one." That other self has dropped away, and now his spiritual Self is shining through.

I *Has Infinite Intelligence and Unlimited Capacity*

There is no question but that parents have some concern as to the degree of intelligence of their children. Every child is pigeonholed in his parent's mind as an *A, B, C, D, E, F,* or something-or-other in conduct and in intellectual accomplishments. They think of that child as brilliant, mediocre, or less than average. They cannot help it, since they are always observing the child from the minute he is born and comparing him with their ideal of perfection. Of course he is not that, and therefore many times they downgrade him right from the beginning. Then the child goes to school and begins to reflect the image his parents have fastened on him.

No one can change a child's intelligence by wanting him to be bright, nor can a bad child be changed into a good one by wanting him to be good. Experience has proved that there is only one way, and that is to let the child drop out of thought for a long enough time to meditate, so that we begin to see *I,* to see that that child is the same *I* that we are. That child is the offspring of the same Father that we are. There is only one creative Principle, one infinite, divine Being, and we are all that divine Being and divine Intelligence in essence and in expression.

As we begin to tabernacle and commune with the spiritual identity of that child, we can watch the change that takes place in his academic accomplishments. Why? Not because we have improved his intellectual capacity, but because we have put aside his lack of intellectual capacity and are drawing forth his Christ-identity. That is what is shining through now in scholastic achievement, attitudes, and behavior.

Christhood, the Only Permanent Relationship

So it is with our neighbors. We are not attempting to improve our neighbors; we are not attempting to make them better persons. That is why we do not proselyte and try to give them what we may think is a better religion. There is no better or best religion. There is only one thing that makes for divine harmony, and that is Christhood. That is the only basis on which we can form a permanent relationship of brotherhood. The only permanent relationship is in our Christhood because no matter how humanly good we may be, some day something is going to come up that touches the personal "I," and then disagreements and conflicts will arise.

This human "I" that responds to a situation by becoming angry with somebody or feeling resentful is the human selfhood that has to be put off. The reason it is difficult to do this is that we sometimes enjoy being angry, and we often get satisfaction out of resentment. When we read about dictators and tyrants, we get pleasure out of thinking about some power that would bring them down and level them out. We all have moments in which we visualize bringing some tyrant to his knees, giving him his comeuppance. But that is the human "I" in us responding, the "I" that has no right to be there at all.

The truth is that I am the embodiment of all the qualities of God. But how dare I make a declaration like that about myself, knowing myself humanly as I do? How dare I make that statement for myself unless I also make it for you? How dare I say that I embody all the God-qualities, that I am as eternal as God, as immortal as God, that I am the Christ-son of God? How dare I say that and leave out any individual anywhere on earth—past, present, or future—any individual in hell or in heaven? I dare not, I dare not! It would be spiritual wickedness to announce my Christhood and refuse to accept the fact that this is a universal truth. God is bidding every individual on the face of the globe to awaken to his true identity. "Awake thou that sleepest!" Christhood is our true identity, not good humanhood, not bad humanhood.

Sooner or later you must be willing to put off this "I" that is full of earthly errors, full of resentments, injustices, inequalities, and declare within yourself, "I am ready to assume my true identity. I am ready to awaken to the light of my own being. I am willing to accept the Master's statement that I am to call no man on earth my father, but acknowledge divine sonship for myself."

Until you can do that for yourself, how can you love your neighbor as yourself? You have not even begun to love yourself. You do not love yourself until you acknowledge your true identity. You are not supposed to love your human self, because even when your human self is good, it is not very good.

Righteous Judgment

It is not your human self that you are to love. You must love only God and His universe, His world, His creation. You must love only God and the offspring of God. You must love only your spiritual identity, because it is your perfected Self. Then, unless you are one of the few madmen of the world who believe that this refers to them exclusively, you will begin to look around at this world and you will realize, "I have been judging after appearances. I have been using the scale of good and evil, the very thing that threw us out of the Garden of Eden. I have been clinging to the very barrier to heaven. Now, judging neither good nor evil, let me judge righteous judgment. And what is righteous judgment except the knowledge of my identity?"

It is not righteous judgment to think of yourself as nearly good, or as three-quarters good. It is not righteous judgment to see a person of thirty and say, "How youthful you are!" and then look at another one of sixty and say, "How old you are getting!" This is not righteous judgment. Righteous judgment is to be able to look at the young and the old and see Christhood, immortality, eternality, spiritual perfection. Then you learn that all these qualities are not yours and mine as personal possessions: they are ours by Grace; they are the gift of God.

That is why humility is always emphasized in a spiritual teaching. Humility means acknowledging that whatever of divine qualities you have, they are not something you have created for yourself: they are something given to you as a gift of God. If you have immortality, if you have eternality, if you have any degree of purity or integrity, it is a God-given gift, but it is a gift to all alike. That here and there are those who are not expressing these gifts, that here and there you and I are not fully expressing them, this has nothing to do with it at the moment.

I *Within You Am Come*

What we are dealing with is truth, and the only truth there is, is the truth about your identity and my identity. When you begin to know yourself as the *I THAT I AM,* the *I* that is one with God, the *I* that has meat the world knows not of, the *I* that is the meat, the wine, and the water, the *I* that is life eternal, then you begin to live a new life, based on this greatest of all revelations: "I am come that they might have life, and that they might have it more abundantly."

From the moment of your recognition of this, your life changes. You are no longer seeking God; you are no longer seeking truth. True, you are seeking a greater realization of the truth you already know, and a greater demonstration of it. But you are no longer seeking God: you now know God, and you know God aright. "I am come that they might have life." This *I* is within you.

That is why the Master could say, "The kingdom of God is within you." Now you do not go around looking for God; you do not look for good. You live in the consciousness of the presence of that *I* within you whose function it is that you live spiritually and eternally. You commune with that *I*.

Drop Humanhood and Realize I

When you turn to your child, your grandchild, your husband, your wife, or your neighbor, you know that the *I* that is within each of them has come that they may be lifted up above all the good the earth has, into a temple not made with hands—into a consciousness not made with hands, into a life not made with hands, into a body not made with hands. All this is the function of the *I* that is within you, the *I* that is within me, and the *I* that is in your child, your grandchild, and other members of your family. Unless you are living with that *I,* you are only trying to pull them apart humanly and make them a little better. Leave their humanhood alone and go inside and realize, "Thank You, Father. *I* in the midst of me am mighty. *I* in the midst of him and her, *I* in the midst of them, *I* in the midst of human consciousness am mighty."

That *I* is the secret of life. That *I* is come so that the whole human race may be lifted up into a temple not made with hands—not just earth with a temporary peace on it, not just earth with an interval between wars, not just earth with a little boom time this year. No, we are to be lifted up through this message into our true consciousness, a consciousness that does not have degrees of good and evil in it. It has only infinite immortality, infinite eternality.

In all these meditations, we have ignored the personal sense of "I" that has problems and wants to get rid of them, and we have brought to light the *I* that we really are, the one that was never born, has no birth date, will never die, and has never had a problem. Red Seas open before that *I.* Manna falls from the sky. Why? Because the *I* lives by Grace—not by might, not by power, by Grace. Without any human effort, everything appears in its order.

In our meditation, we must always remember that we are that temple not made with hands. That enables us to shut the physical body out and to go right through any appearance to the *I* at the center of our being.

CHAPTER X

AN ACT OF COMMITMENT

As I sat in meditation these words came to me, "the womb of Silence," and with them it was as if there were a tremendous silence, large and round, and this was the Womb out of which all creation came.* All creation was formed in this womb of Silence. There was not a man, but there was a universe: the earth, the rocks, the trees, streams, seas, skies, suns, moons, and planets—all this flowing forth as an unfoldment from this huge Womb of penetrating, complete stillness—yet more than stillness: absolute silence, quietness.

It moves as if in a rhythm, and this rhythm not only forms it, but sustains creation with everything in its rightful place. Looking out into this universe, you can see that there is cold—snow and ice—in the north and warmth in the south, flowers and trees of one nature in the north and of another in the south. This rhythm, the rhythm that is flowing from that Silence, maintains and sustains creation beautifully, all in its order.

*The meditation referred to immediately preceded the third hour of the 1964 London Studio Class, June 14, 1964—Ed.

Eventually, man appears here and there on the face of the globe, also maintained by this rhythm that flows within his consciousness. It is a flow of rhythm that maintains the activity of the body, the organs and their functions. Everything seems to be responsive to this rhythm, and all this rhythm is flowing forth from that Womb into form as grace, beauty, order, peace. The relationship between all these forms is harmonious. We could use the words "love" or "loving," but there is no love or loving. There is only a naturalness of peace, contentment, and this is the rhythm in expression, the rhythm of the universe.

Inharmony Results from Being Outside the Rhythm

When anything goes wrong in our experience, it is because we are out of tune with this rhythm. We can observe the willow tree, how it moves with the breeze, almost flows with the breeze, and then imagine what would happen if it were to try to stand erect in that breeze or resist it. It would be broken. And so is man broken the moment he is moving outside the rhythm, outside the flow that brought him into manifestation and expression.

The rhythm from the Source maintains all creation in harmony, in law and order, and whatever it is that permits us to move in a way of our own or with a will of our own, a direction of our own, removes us from the flow of the rhythm, and then we are either in opposition to it or trying to stand erect in the face of it. Every sense of discord and inharmony that touches our experience is an evidence that we are out of alignment or out of attunement with the rhythm of the universe, and discord and inharmony are going to persist in our experience until we are once more spiritually, rhythmically attuned.

How to Return to the Rhythm

There may not be a possibility at this moment of explaining why or how we get out of attunement, but the acknowledgment must be made that as a human race we are not being governed by the rhythm of the Spirit, the rhythm of the Silence. It may very well be that it is because we insist on taking thought: we insist on a way of our own, a will of our own, a family strictly of our own, instead of recognizing the oneness of all life. It could well be that we will come partly back into the rhythm by acknowledging that there is only one family and that we are of the household of God, thereby uniting ourselves with the peoples of all races, of all religions, and of all nationalities. Acknowledging the common fatherhood of God would in one way restore harmony.

Another way shows us the wisdom of tithing. But this practice must not be misunderstood. This ancient teaching of tithing did not mean that if we tithed we could expect some blessing. We cannot enter into any merchandising or bargaining arrangement with God so that we give 10 per cent and He gives back 90. But by tithing in the sense of acknowledging our relationship, not merely to our own flesh and blood, but acknowledging our relationship to all mankind, we place ourselves in the rhythm of that relationship. In providing for others in addition to our own, we are not merely intellectually acknowledging a relationship, but are living in the rhythm of it. We are in the rhythm of our relationship to mankind when, first of all, we acknowledge that relationship, and then act on it by making some measure of provision for others outside our own flesh-and-blood household, our own religious household, or our own national household.

The Universal Relationship of Mankind Must Be Acknowledged by an Act

Is it clear that to reestablish ourselves in this original rhythm it becomes necessary to do it by an act? Intellectual knowledge is not sufficient: it must be followed by an act. This is a commitment; this is an act of commitment. If we declare that we are all of the household of God and then continue to live only for our own family, for those of our own religion or our own nation, we are virtually contradicting ourselves and setting up a friction, and our condition is then worse than that of the person who is ignorant of this universal relationship.

Once we acknowledge this universal relationship by an act of commitment, we must enter into the rhythm and begin to act in some way that will commit us to the welfare of those others outside the relationship of our home, community, nation, or church. If we merely acknowledge our Christhood, instead of living out from that Christhood by an act, we at once set up a conflict within our own being that is far worse than if we had never heard of Christhood, because having heard of It, we must now live It.

There must be an act of commitment in which we live as the Christ, and in order to understand that we may take such examples as Gautama the Buddha and Jesus the Christ, and witness the nature of the life they lived. It is not that we are going to equal their life. That, of course, can never be. Each of us is an individual, and we unfold individually. But at least we can see what is meant by accepting one's Christhood, and then make a beginning by doing something, even if it is a very little "unto . . . the least of these my brethren," so that this little that we do may continue to increase in scope, depth, breadth, and vision.

The Acknowledgment of the Christhood of Our Fellow Man Must Be Expressed in Action

To acknowledge the Christhood of our fellow man is to bring forth another act of commitment. Not only must I act out from the acknowledgment of my Christhood insofar as the light is given me, but in the moment that I recognize the Christ of you, I am then called upon to act toward you as if you were the Christ. As I bow my head in the presence of the Master, so do I bow my head in the presence of everyone I meet.

Very often students wonder if their spiritual teacher is aware of the nature or the degree of their spiritual unfoldment or lack of it. They may be assured that it is as impossible to hide their degree of spiritual unfoldment from the teacher as it would be to hide from God, because there is a sign, and that sign is an act of commitment. Until the teacher observes that sign, he knows exactly how far spiritual development has proceeded. The moment he witnesses the sign of commitment, he knows that the student has gone over the hump, has reached a place beyond humanhood. But this is not until that act of commitment in one form or another is observed. It does not have to be observed physically. One does not have to be within thousands of miles of the student to know when the commitment has taken place.

Our Individual Consciousness Is the Judge

This brings us to an important part of The Infinite Way unfoldment. It is not difficult to convince a person that he can get away with evil and be undetected by God, but we could do away with all the prisons on earth if it were correctly taught that no one gets away with anything because the judge is closer than breathing: it is one's very own consciousness.

The judge does not act as many people have believed that God acts, sitting with a ledger writing down the good deeds and the bad deeds and weighing them against each other. But rather it acts like the law of mathematics. As long as we keep putting two times two together and getting four, three times three and getting nine, all is going well within our mathematical kingdom. Nobody is being rewarded; mathematics is not being rewarded, and numbers are not being rewarded. It is just that all is well as the normal natural unfoldment of the laws of mathematics or science. On the other hand, if we put two times two together and get five, we do not receive any punishment: we merely have broken the rhythm of harmony. Nobody is being punished; the numbers are not being punished, and arithmetic is not being punished. There is just the erroneous fruitage from breaking the rhythm of mathematics.

H_2O is water, and as long as we keep putting H_2O together, we get water, but it will not be as a reward from God: it will be the normal natural rhythm of the divine order of science. Try to put $H\frac{1}{2}O$ together, and we do not get water (in fact, no such formula or substance exists), but no one is being punished—not even the scientist who makes the mistake. The rhythm has merely been broken.

Violating Spiritual Law Breaks the Rhythm

Every time we violate spiritual law, the rhythm is broken, and we violate spiritual law every time that we do not acknowledge God as Omnipotence, Omniscience, Omnipresence, and every time that we do not love our neighbor as ourselves. These are the only two spiritual commandments there are. This is the rhythm of the entire created universe including man.

There is no way to violate the rhythm except to accept two powers: good and evil in the place of the omnipotence of Spirit; to accept a mind other than the mind of God; to accept a presence other than the presence of God. To do that breaks the rhythm. No one breaks it for us. As long as we are in obedience to acknowledging God in all our ways, knowing Him aright as the one and only Power, the one and only Presence, the one and only Intelligence, and loving our neighbor as ourselves, acknowledging the Christhood of ourselves, acknowledging the Christhood of our neighbor, and then acting out that love, "no weapon that is formed against [us] shall prosper." If anyone tries to send a weapon at us, he destroys himself, if we know this truth.

On the other hand, the moment we violate these commandments, the law is broken, and then whatever discord or inharmony comes we ourselves have set in motion. We have done this by a violation of the only two commandments that exist in the spiritual kingdom. What about stealing? What about committing adultery? Is it not clear that if we are honoring our neighbor as the Christ we would hardly be stealing from him or committing adultery? Such acts would not come under the spiritual law of loving our neighbor as ourselves.

The Rhythm of the Universe Provides All Things Necessary

There is a rhythm, and this rhythm of the universe makes each one of us an individual, an individual completely governed and fulfilled by the Spirit of God, with all things provided for us in accord with the need of every particular moment, so that we never have to envy our neighbor, be jealous or lustful, because in the rhythm our own will come to us.

This is what John Burroughs really said in his poem, "Waiting." This poem is very much misunderstood, and there are many persons who believe that all they have to do is to sit and wait, and their own will come to them. There are those who have been waiting a whole lifetime, and it has not happened yet, because they are still in that human state of consciousness which is outside the rhythm of the universe. But John Burroughs was speaking from the Spirit Itself, and since he was in the rhythm of the Spirit, he was observing that our own will come to us and we do not have to seek it. We sit by the side of the stream, and our own comes.

As long as we are in the flow of obedience to loving God supremely, acknowledging the infinite *I,* the infinite Consciousness as the only Power, the only Presence, the only Wisdom, loving our neighbor as ourselves, doing unto our neighbor as we would have our neighbor do unto us, we are living in the rhythm.

Sitting in the silence, acknowledging the *I* of my being, acknowledging omniscient, omnipotent Omnipresence is the way. This is the way of restoring harmony, but always it must be accompanied by an act of commitment.

Silence Is the Womb of Creation

We must have our realization and our act of reliance. But then we cannot separate this loving of God supremely from loving our neighbor as ourselves as if they were two separate commandments. They are virtually two parts of one commandment. If we were to acknowledge God but not love our neighbor as ourselves, our formula would not work. We must acknowledge the flow of this rhythm from the Silence that we enter which is the Womb from which all creation flows. The Silence that we attain within is the Womb, and out of this Silence within flows all creation as it is necessary to our individual experience.

With it flows the loving of our neighbor as ourselves. That comes quickly, but then it must be acted upon. There must be an act of commitment, an "inasmuch as ye have done it unto one of the least of these my brethren, ye have done it unto" yourself; or "inasmuch as ye did it not to one of the least of these," ye have not done it unto yourself.

We cheat ourselves by not doing unto our neighbor, for our neighbor is our Self. If we are limiting our neighbor to our relatives, countrymen, fellow religionists, we are cheating our Self, because it is only as we do unto another that we have done it unto the Self of us.

The rhythm of the universe is made up of the acknowledgment of *I* as God, Omniscience, Omnipotence, Omnipresence, and by an act of commitment. The loving of our neighbor as ourselves is an act of commitment. There must be dedication and devotion to this principle, not to persons, but to this principle. It should not make any difference to us whether the Russians get the benefit of our benefactions or the Chinese or the Cubans. What must concern us is our act of commitment to those outside our family circle of nations, of allies, or of friends.

Consciousness Projecting Itself

Man shall live by the Word, not merely by bread. As we receive the Word flowing from our consciousness through the Silence and perform an act of commitment that binds and relates us to It, that identifies us with It, then we have come out from the rest of the world and become separate. Our world is an emanation of our state of consciousness. The higher our state of consciousness rises in obedience to the two commandments, the more joyous, peaceful, and harmonious becomes the created world, because the created world is a creation of our consciousness.

If we could see or feel that behind our head was this great Consciousness projecting Itself, and then if we did not get in Its way by taking thought, this Consciousness would flow in Its infinite form and variety, and there would be no limitation to our universe or its harmony. It is only as we in some measure get in the way of this flow with that personal sense of "I," "me," and "mine" that our universe is a bit less infinite than it should be.

You may believe that you are following this Infinite Way of life by reading the books or hearing the message, but I say that you are not, until you have arrived at the place of an act of commitment. You may believe that you are under the law of God, but I say that you are not, until you have brought yourself there by an act of commitment. You may believe that God's grace is going to take care of you, and I say that it is not, until you have been brought to a place of commitment.

The Reason for Meditation

From this, you can see the importance of meditation, a meditation which is not a stopping of thought, not a deadening of consciousness, nor an escaping from the world, but a meditation in which the darkness or the silence is so great that you can look through it and see the whole of infinite Consciousness behind you, ready to pour Itself forth into your expectant inner ear as you invite It to "speak, Lord; for thy servant heareth."

You can almost feel that great, great area of Consciousness behind you, pushing and pushing, sending Itself forth into expression through your consciousness, as your consciousness, as the Word, as the still small voice, over and over repeating, "*I* am come that you might have life. *I* am come that you might *have.* Take no thought for your life. *I* am come."

And then you say, "Ah, that is why I have hidden manna; that is why I have meat the world knows not of. I have this *I* in the depth of this inner stillness and darkness, in the depth of this inner womb of Silence. There is *I.* 'Be still, and know that I am God.' This is the hidden manna. This is the meat the world knows not of. This is the manna that I must keep sacred and secret, sharing only as those who come to me are ready."

Do not think for a moment that you can turn to this rhythm of the Spirit just to have your life made healthy, wealthy, and wise. There is no provision for that in the spiritual kingdom. You turn within that the word of God may flow through you to this world. You will be taken care of, certainly. "The way that provides not for the wayfarer is no way to fare upon."* This way of *I* does provide for us. But that is not the reason that we meditate.

The reason we meditate is that the kingdom of God may be established on earth as it is in heaven. God forbid that we should want the kingdom of God on earth for us alone. This would be very much like persons who buy bombproof shelters for their protection, and then after the world has been blown up, come out and find that they are the only people left on earth. Imagine what kind of a lonesome world that is going to be for them—a hell on earth. Or it is like the people who are stocking their bombproof shelters with food, and when it is all over they expect to come out and find that

*Mikhail Naimy, *The Book of Mirdad* (Bombay: N. M. Tripathi, 1954), p. 15.

nobody else has food except themselves. Can you imagine their being able to eat a bite of it?

The Illumined: Masters or Servants?

We do not meditate that we may find our peace, but that through us peace may flow to the world. Moses did not receive his enlightenment that he might become a glorious king, but that he might go right down to the valley with his Hebrew people and suffer with them in bringing them forth into freedom. Guatama the Buddha did not receive his enlightenment to be set apart on a mountaintop and bowed down to and worshiped, but that he might walk the length and breadth of India, teaching disciples and establishing healing ashramas. Jesus Christ did not receive his enlightenment that he might be set apart from the rest of the world to sing hymns and play harps while the rest of the world was in slavery. To no man is it given to be enlightened for his own sake. It has never happened in the history of the world.

And yet there are thousands and thousands of people who are seeking enlightenment, seeking illumination, believing that when they receive it they are going to be healthy, wealthy, and wise forever after, all by themselves. No, let us have no such illusions. If you are seeking enlightenment, you will receive it as long as you are not dreaming of it as setting you apart from the world or as making you a master on earth.

Illumination will make you a servant. Other people may call you a master, but in your heart you will be smiling, "You call me master, but I know the extent to which I am a servant. I know the extent to which I am called upon to serve. All the rest of the world seems to be my master." No, illumination does not bring fancy titles or robes, or a life of peace set apart: it brings a life of dedication, of devotion, of service.

When the Master told his disciples to leave their nets, he was asking for a sign of commitment, and if they received illumination from him it was only that they should become "fishers of men."

Read the story of the life of Paul and notice the whippings, the imprisonments, and the hunger he endured in order to carry the message of the Christ to mankind. Examine the lives of all the mystics and see the misunderstandings and sometimes imprisonments that were their lot. Illumination carries a price: leave the world, leave mother, brother, sister, and father if necessary for *My* sake. Be assured that if there is illumination there is an act of commitment to the entire world, not just to a sect and not just to a community. It is not merely setting up office hours three hours a day, three days a week. To receive illumination and dedication means an act of commitment to the world seven days a week, twenty-four hours a day.

God does not reveal Himself lightly, or for selfish purposes, or to those who would use God. The pure in heart are those who understand the nature of the two commandments as constituting the rhythm of the universe, and in obedience to those two commandments, they are in attunement with the rhythm of the universe as it flows from the silence that they attain within themselves. "In quietness and in confidence shall be your strength." Be still and know that *I* in the midst of you am God. Be still and let the rhythm flow from that Silence within your own being, and then follow it with the act of commitment that aligns you with the people of this world.

If anyone's name is to survive as a spiritual leader or teacher, it must be that of an individual who has come into attunement with the Spirit of God, which is the Spirit of all mankind, of all men and all women and all children everywhere. It leaves no one out. There is a Spirit in man, and it is to This that we attune ourselves, and then receive fruitage as we attain the state of consciousness that enables us to make the act of commitment. Whether it is to leave our nets, to sell all that we have to purchase the pearl, or to leave mother and father, there is an act of commitment that unites us with God and man.

CHAPTER XI

AN ACT OF WORSHIP AND THE FRUITAGE

We live and move and have our being in a sea of Consciousness, an infinite ocean of Consciousness, pouring Itself through and as our individual consciousness, and appearing outwardly as form. As long as we do not get in Its way with "I," "me," or "mine," the rhythm of that Consciousness will continue to unfold harmoniously. The outer appearances, the outer forms, will be harmonious ones, and we will be living the spiritual life, living in the Fourth Dimension of life.

If we violate a moral or a spiritual law, we have set in motion karmic law, the law of as-ye-sow-so-shall-ye-reap. Sooner or later, our error will find us out and demand payment. This we have come to look upon as punishment, almost as if it were punishment from God. As a matter of fact, most religions teach that the punishment is from God.

When the world learns the truth that is revealed in *The Thunder of Silence,** it will discover that this is not true. Any punishment we

*By the author (New York: Harper and Row, 1961).

receive is not punishment from God any more than believing that two times two is five and then thinking that any unpleasant effects from this erroneous belief are a punishment from God. The punishment is not from God: it is due entirely to our ignorance; and the punishment ends in the very moment of our enlightenment.

As long as we continue to live as human beings, there is no setting aside of karmic law, even if we were to wait ten generations. Karmic law, however, is set aside in any given moment when we return to the rhythm of the universe by bringing ourselves into attunement with, and by obedience to, the two great commandments: "Love the Lord thy God with all thy heart, and with all thy soul, and with all thy mind," and "Love thy neighbor as thyself." These two commandments are not easy to follow. Most of us have discovered that it is impossible to love the Lord our God with all our heart and with all our soul, and it is even more impossible to love our neighbor as ourselves. Personally, I feel that if anyone claims that he is doing that, he is lying, except under one condition, and that is if he knows the meaning of loving God and if he knows the meaning of loving his neighbor.

Loving God and loving our neighbor have nothing whatsoever to do with any emotion. Neither of these has to do with love in any way that we understand love, unless we can translate the word "love" into obedience to the law.

Living Out from Omniscience, Omnipotence, and Omnipresence

To "love the Lord thy God with all thy heart, and with all thy soul, and with all thy mind" means to acknowledge God as Omniscience, thereby learning to refrain from asking or telling God or demanding anything of God. It means to observe silence in the presence of God and to accept God as Omnipotence. We are never to seek the power of God, for in the realization of Omnipotence and Omnipresence, there is no time or place in all of history where a power has been needed.

In the recognition of Omniscience, there is a demand for silence in the presence of God. In the recognition of Omnipotence, there is a demand for silence in the presence of God. In the recognition of Omnipresence, there is also a demand for silence. The only form of prayer acceptable to God is absolute silence, a relaxing and a resting in the conviction of God as Omniscience, Omnipotence, and Omnipresence. To bring forth the grace of God, the glory and the perfection of God, it is necessary to be still, so that in that stillness the rhythm of the universe can flow forth as harmony.

Uniting All Men in the Household of God

You will soon see what an act of commitment it is to be able to cease from taking thought, to be able to refrain from reminding God of your needs, or seeking the help of God. This is indeed an act of commitment—a difficult one, too, very difficult. But just as entering the silence in the presence of God is an act of commitment, so is this further requirement of loving "thy neighbor as thyself," and in order for that rhythm of the universe to come forth as harmony, that additional act of commitment must be made.

The meaning of "love thy neighbor" is not too difficult to grasp. In its essence, does it not mean the breaking down of the barriers of family, national, and religious affiliations, and the uniting of all men in the household of God? Does it not demand the breaking up of all national, racial , and religious prejudices and agreeing on the one family of God: God the Father of all?

Whether we are providing food for other nations, even enemy nations, or education for children other than our own, or at least contributing toward it, or whatever else we may do of an unselfed nature for our fellow man, this is the act that proves our acceptance of the commandment to love our neighbor as ourselves. This is the act of commitment confirming our inner agreement. When this has been completed, we are in obedience to the law of God, we are children of God, and now the rhythm of God can flow through us without interruption, without hitting up against barriers, without being deflected, and we can become beholders.

Recognizing Our Neighbor As Our Self

"The world is new to every soul when Christ has entered into it."* The mystery has always been: When does Christ enter in, or how do we bring Christ in? And here we have the answer. Christ enters in, in the moment our consciousness is purged of its belief in two powers, purged of the hatred, envy, and jealousy that sets man apart from man. As soon as the rhythm of the universe is functioning within us, the Christ has entered our soul and the world becomes new, because not only are we loving our neighbor—we may never have an emotion such as loving our neighbor—but we are loving our neighbor *concretely,* and in doing this our neighbor is compelled to love us. Thereby, we deprive our neighbor of the power of not loving us.

It would seem, humanly, that we do not have the power to deprive others of their power to injure us, but we do, we do. We make it an impossibility to be misunderstood or mistreated because there is only one Self, and that which takes place as the consciousness of my Self takes place as the consciousness of your Self because of our acknowledgment of one Self. In the moment that I love my neighbor as myself, I make my neighbor's consciousness and my consciousness one and the same consciousness, responding therefore to the same influence.

By loving my neighbor as myself, I deprive this world of its ability to send weapons against me. But this, too, is an act of commitment.

*Quoted from an inscription in the chapel at Stanford University, Palo Alto, Calif., in the author's *The World Is New* (New York: Harper & Row, 1961), p. 7.

This is an act of commitment, however, that does not take place on one day and then forever after absolve us from further responsibility. No, it is an act of commitment that takes place not only every day of our life, but usually many times in each day. Every time we meet a person, it compels us to another act of commitment because the human mesmerism is such that we would automatically set this individual as one apart from the others to whom we have been previously committed.

Continuous Acts of Commitment Speed the "Death" of Personal Sense

Of course, you see that this resolves itself finally into "dying daily" to that personal sense of "I" but do not believe for a moment that you can "die" completely to that word "I." It would seem that on this plane that is an impossibility. There may come a time when the Christ is raised so high in our consciousness that the little "I" disappears, but if it has ever happened we have no record of it.

We know that the personal sense of "I" was present with Jesus when he was preaching against the officials of the church and the money changers, those in high places, those who demanded animal sacrifice. We know that the personal sense of "I" was there when he asked his disciples, "Could ye not watch with me one hour?"

So it is not likely that in our earthly span we will entirely die out of a personal sense of "I," but we can minimize the effects of the personal sense of "I" by continuous acts of commitment in the loving of God with all our heart, soul, and mind, and in the loving of our neighbor as ourselves.

A Reason for Our Faith

As we continue to do this and retire into the silence in the presence of God, the rhythm flows forth. Do not, however, make the mistake many of those on the spiritual path have made. Do not permit yourself to lapse into blind faith. It is quite right to have faith in two times two being four or to have faith in H_2O being water, but do not have a faith in "ye know not what," for this is dangerous.

Therefore, when you are in the silence in the presence of God and you are expecting this rhythm of life to flow forth through your consciousness as harmony in the outer world, be sure that you have a reason for your faith. That reason is that we have come into the awareness that *I* is the name of God. We have agreed that that is why we can be still and know that *I* in the midst of us is God.

Then we see why it is true that I have hidden manna, why I have meat the world knows not of, why I have the Source, the Fountainhead, the Storehouse which *I* am. And because the infinity of life, the immortality of life, is stored up in the *I* which I am, I can be still and let that rhythm flow out, going before me, walking beside me, behind me, and appearing when necessary as a cloud by day and a pillar of fire by night, as a poor widow sharing, as cakes baked on the stone, or as the multiplication of loaves and fishes.

The Miracle Is Silence

Here again I repeat a former lesson: Do not believe that there are miracle workers on earth, that any *man* can multiply loaves and fishes or make manna fall from the sky, or water come from rocks. There is no provision in the entire kingdom of God for this. Be still and know that *I* can give you water. That *I,* you remember, is that presence of God before which we are silent. Just know that *I* can multiply loaves and fishes—that *I* before which we stand in complete silence. Then we can be beholders as loaves and fishes are multiplied. We can behold living waters flowing, healing waters, curative waters. We can behold the word of God coming forth as bread, meat, and wine. We can behold the word of God appearing outwardly as an activity of divine Grace.

But only remember this, and never forget it: no man on the face of the globe can perform a miracle except the miracle of silence. For most of us, this is itself a miracle if we are able to attain it. Be still for the space of a second, and then you will see the *I,* which we do not use or manipulate, but which we behold in stillness and quietness, in silence. This *I* appears outwardly as harmony in our experience. It even appears as a power which shuts the lion's mouth and stops the Pilates of this world.

When Scripture says, "Greater is he that is in you, than he that is in the world," do you see exactly how much greater, how much mightier? The might of God is within us, and that mightiness can be brought into the external realm by our taking the attitude of a beholder and being completely still in the presence of the *I* that we are.

Karmic Law Is Broken As Personal Sense Is Withdrawn

It is this *I* that our thoughts hit up against when the human part of us indulges in the human hates, human loves, human fears, human doubts, and human ignorance. When these hit up against that *I,* they rebound as what we call punishment. Is this punishment, or is it just the natural error that is born of error?

Karmic law, the law of as-ye-sow-so-shall-ye-reap, is set in motion whenever human sentiment hits up against the spiritual reality of the *I* that I am. The moment we think a wrong thought or do a wrong deed, this hits up against our own inner spiritual integrity and bounces back at us. Because the results are not always visible at the moment, we sometimes think we can escape them, but inevitably they reach us, and then we wonder afterwards, "Why do I suffer from this? Why did this have to happen to me?" We have forgotten the law that we set in motion by violating our own spiritual integrity. Fortunately, we can correct this at any time by withdrawing the personal sense of self that loves, hates, or fears, and by becoming beholders as we stand in the presence of the Spirit, the *I* that is within us. This absolves us from all our previous mistakes and the penalties thereof.

Forgiveness Comes When the I *Dissolves Personal Sense*

There is no use in asking for forgiveness for our mistakes because there is this spiritual integrity, the integrity of the *I* which is the All-knowing, and It already knows whether that other "I" has been dissolved. When a cloud obscures the sun, the sun does not reach the earth, but when the cloud is dispersed the sun again shines on earth. Did the sun know the cloud was there to prevent its reaching the earth? Did the sun ever stop shining?

So it is that this *I* at the center of your being and my being is your individual spiritual integrity and mine, and it is always shining. Then a cloud gets in the way. And what is the nature of that cloud? Personal sense, the human sense of "I." But this infinite integrity which is mine, which *I* am, keeps right on shining, and in the course of time, as Scripture says, "Every knee shall bow," and this means that every cloud must eventually be dispelled.

The light which *I* am dispels all personal sense, and then "the glory which I had with thee before the world was" is in full evidence to the world, and the world says, "This is the glory of the Lord." But That which we are does not know that It is burning away the dross of the personal sense of you and of me which we entertain. It does not know it. Our spiritual integrity is just shining, and sooner or later that dross will evaporate, and the *I* which we are will not know that there ever was a personal sense of "I" to be forgiven. There is no use saying, "Please forgive me," because as long as there is a "me" to ask forgiveness, there is no forgiveness, but when there is a longing heart leaning toward forgiveness, this is that right motive that is the purification process.

We honor God and we honor our spiritual integrity when, instead of asking for forgiveness or favors, we approach God with the finger on the lips and on the mind, going to God without thoughts, without desires, going to this center within ourselves in silence that we may hear the still small voice even when it is at its stillest and smallest.

God's Love Cannot Be Channeled

The listening ear is the attitude in prayer and meditation: that we may hear, *not that we may be heard,* only that we may hear, that we may receive impartations from within. We do this with the full knowledge that we are not going to receive God's grace for any personal purpose or use, but that it is for the benefit of all. If we are going to pray for God's grace, let us pray for it as a universal benediction that the kingdom of God may be established on earth as it is in heaven; for whatever we may think, say, or do, it is going to be that way. It is not going to be any other way. No one can channel God's love to this nation or that nation, to this family or that family, to this person or that person. God's love cannot be channeled: God's love is for the unjust as well as the just.

Jesus could not condemn anyone for his sins, knowing that they were the remnant of the personal sense of self that was left. On the other hand, he could not tolerate anyone calling him good, knowing as he did the source of that good, and certainly Jesus would have been just as rebellious had anyone commented on his great miracle works in multiplying loaves and fishes, for he well knew that no man is a miracle worker.

Forgiveness Comes in a Moment of Commitment

God has not given it to any man to be a miracle worker, but man in his silence becomes the transparency for the miracle-working Spirit Itself. Without this, an egotism would spring up that would forever dam up that Spirit within. If ever we could be made to believe that mortal man is or can be spiritual, or that mortal man is or can be the child of God, then all the stupidity would follow that has made people believe that they can go to church on Sunday, and by some hocus-pocus be forgiven and then begin their deviltries all over again on Monday, still carrying with them their lack of charity, their lack of benevolence, their lack of forgiveness, or their lack of brotherliness. How could they then be purified?

The Hebrews taught, and still do, that on one day a year, by observing the rituals and rites of that day, they are forgiven. But this is impossible. No one is forgiven that which he has in his consciousness which is unlike God. It cannot be forgiven: it has to be forsaken. When it is forsaken, it does not exist and does not have to be forgiven. Therefore the only forgiveness is when the transcendent Spirit enters and purifies us, and that need not be on a certain day of the year. It happens at a certain moment, and usually a moment of commitment.

The Power Is Not in Words but in Consciousness

Do not rely on words, mantrams, or prayers. If words and thoughts come they are but the tools, the working tools. The power is in the consciousness through which the words come. God is individual consciousness. That is why we sit in silence with the listening ear, without words and without thoughts, in the presence of the *I* that I am. Out of that still consciousness comes the Word that is power. It may come as a great many words and thoughts, but do not hold onto the words and thoughts, because then you lose the power.

Learn to sit in an attitude of respect, love, and gratitude before the door of your own consciousness. Ah yes, remember this: *I* stand at the door of your consciousness. "I stand at the door, and knock." Do you not see that *I* can enter only as you settle into this peaceful, quiet listening before the door of your own consciousness? Do not make the mistake of worshiping somebody else's consciousness, somebody of the past, present, or hoped-for future. Learn to understand that *I* stand at the door of every consciousness, saint and sinner, and as you learn to sit in respectful silence, *I* will open Itself to you, will reveal Itself as power, presence, meat, wine, and water.

The words you think will never multiply loaves and fishes. The thoughts you think will never heal anyone of his ills. The power is in the Consciousness, and when It utters Itself the earth melts. There must be a "you" and a "me" sitting at the feet of the Master, but sitting where at the feet of the Master? Sitting inside our own consciousness, in silence, in secrecy, telling no man what we are doing, and there receiving the bread, the wine, the meat, the water, the Word.

Listening Is the Correct Attitude for Prayer

There is not God *and* man. There is no God answering prayer from above or outside, and be assured there is no grace of God to error; praying for God's grace, while still indulging the personal sense of self and of the world, is like asking the illiterate to work out a problem in higher mathematics.

There is no use in trying to claim spirituality for one's self; there is no use in trying to claim Christhood or Godhood for one's self. The far better approach to the spiritual life is to sit in the silence before your own consciousness and let the Voice tell you who you are, what you are, when, where, how much, how little, and why.

Make no claims for yourself, since those claims will not stand up before your inner integrity. They will make a liar of you. Keep the finger on the lips: "If I'm a saint, fine, God did it. If I'm a sinner, it's too bad; I can't help it. But let me in either case, saint or sinner, just sit here at the feet of the Master within myself, and let the Father reveal to me my identity, the nature of my being; and as the Light of the world, let the Father pierce the clouds that would come between me and spiritual demonstration."

Silently, sacredly, secretly, not to be seen of men, not to act outwardly as if we were other than all men, but inwardly always sitting at the feet of the Master, let our prayer be, "Speak, Lord; for thy servant heareth." The effect of this prayer is that the Lord does not tell us our faults, but the Lord dissolves them.

In all my years in the teaching and healing ministry, I have never yet had God tell me about an error in any person. I have witnessed a great many errors dissolved in other persons as well as in myself, but I have never heard God tell me that anyone had an error.

Speaking to God and thinking thoughts up to God is a pure waste of time. Anything we say or think would be bound to hit up against our inner spiritual integrity and bounce back at us because the truth is not in us as human beings. But to maintain a complete attitude of receptivity to the Word that is imparted to us, this is the attitude of prayer, the attitude of meditation, the attitude of healing, the attitude of being a beholder of God's miracles. I know that more and more Oriental literature is going to be read as time goes on, and more and more self-delusion is going to take place through misinterpreting it, believing that there are miracle workers, but there are no miracle workers. Anyone through whom miracles take place is but a transparency through whom the Spirit performs the miracle.

This is It.

CHAPTER XII

DO NOT "PASS BY ON THE OTHER SIDE"

The unveiling of God takes place within you when you realize that it is the *I* in the midst of you that is God, in whom you can relax without words and without thoughts, relax and receive the Word, rest and receive His Spirit, rest in His grace with no concern for tomorrow and no regrets about yesterday, no living over of the yesterdays in your memory, for these have been erased.

When God is unveiled in you, you begin to live in the nowness of life. It is as if you awakened each morning and realized that God has given you a new day. It is a day that will be filled with something. It is a day that you can choose to fill with His presence, with His Spirit, with His love; or it is a day that you can fill with human belief —material laws and mental laws—if you ignore the presence of the Spirit of God in you.

Scripture cannot be fulfilled yesterday, and Scripture will not be fulfilled tomorrow. Scripture is fulfilled in this day, if so be you accept the "unveiling" and let the Spirit of God teach you, let the Spirit of God feed and inspire you, let the Spirit of God walk with you through every minute of every day, and never attempt to walk through even a minute alone. The "unveiling" comes in that moment of your decision to awaken in the morning with God, to fall asleep at night with God, and to determine that every minute of every day you will walk with God and let God walk in you and through you.

That is the goal, and the means of attaining this goal is the attentive ear, the listening ear. You are walking with God and living with and in God only as you learn to keep an open ear throughout your waking and sleeping hours. For a while it may be necessary to open your ears the very last thing at night and say, "Speak, Lord; for thy servant heareth," and then sleep. When you fall asleep this way, your body and mind are at rest, but you yourself are awake. You will then be receiving thoughts throughout the night just as consciously as you do throughout the day.

In that state of consciousness, you will be aware of the events taking place in the spiritual kingdom and sometimes of their relationship to you in your earthly affairs, because *I* never slumbers or sleeps. Consciousness never sleeps, never lapses into unconsciousness; and Consciousness is what I am. The mind and body are what I use, but Consciousness is what I am.

Before there was ever a concept of God, you can be assured there was *I AM,* and *I* was there, and *I* am there, and *I* will be there. *I* in the beginning had all the glory of God, with God, and in God, and therefore *I* had no need to create in my mind a God to worship. In the beginning, *I* already was endowed from on high with His grace, robed in His Spirit, clothed in His immortality. Thus enfolded in His grace, there was no sin, no disease, no death, and therefore no need to invent a God to get rid of these.

God is needed in the mind of man only when he is experiencing some lack or limitation, or some error or evil. A child does not need

God, because the child is living in all his innocence of being, already being all that a child should be. Nothing need be added to the child, and he knows it. Many children have told their parents that they commune inwardly with God, indicating that they were born with an understanding of the true nature of God. They have discovered a God that is not an idea or thought in the mind of a human being but rather an experience of consciousness, an inner communion in the Soul.

God's Grace Is for the Benefit of All Men

When God is unveiled for you so that you behold God as the Soul of all mankind, you can actually feel within you that the Christ is incarnate in you, in me, and in your neighbor: friendly neighbor, enemy neighbor, Christian neighbor, Jewish neighbor, pagan neighbor, atheistic neighbor. When God is revealed in your consciousness as Omnipresence, as that Spirit which is in you, and when you never again ask God for anything, plead with God, tell God what you want, but abide always in the consciousness of God-presence, then you have experienced God, and God is unveiled for you.

God is universal. Just as God has provided a sun in the sky that shines on all lands and all seas, so the grace of God is meant universally for all men. When a Krishna received a revelation of God's presence and God's grace, it was not that some man might be lifted up and worshiped as if he were a special son of God, but rather that through him the knowledge of God might be given to those of his particular world and age. When a Jesus Christ appeared on earth it was not that he might walk about this earth set apart from mankind, but that God appearing as the consciousness of Jesus Christ might be a light unto his world.

So it is also that when the message of The Infinite Way was given to me, it was only that through me this message could be brought to the entire world. Can you, then, believe that it is possible for you to receive a message which is to be a great blessing only to you and probably your family? At first it may appear so, but do not be fooled by appearances. If you have been prepared by the Spirit to receive a spiritual message or teaching, it is only that, through you, it may be spread out into your world. It may begin with the world of your family; it may begin with the world of your community; but it must go on and on until that message finds its way into human consciousness universally.

The Joy of a Spiritual Relationship

Those who have worked with the message of The Infinite Way for any length of time have received benefits of one nature or another, although not always in accord with what they were at first seeking. Sometimes a person comes to a spiritual teaching with the idea of quickly gaining health, and then probably finds that health is the very last thing he attains. Others may come in the hope of finding happiness or prosperity, and they, too, may discover that these are the very last blessings that come to them. But each one discovers that it does not take long before blessings in some form or other begin to appear in his experience, and so he clings and clings to the message until eventually he does perceive the fullness of Grace.

No one who has ever received benefits through the understanding and practice of this message, however, can even begin to know the blessings of it until he has come into association with other students, and especially with students from many parts of the world, from friendly countries, so-called, and from enemy countries, so-called. Those of you who have had that experience have discovered for yourselves the bond of oneness that exists among the students of this work. This is not by virtue of any human relationship or human tie, for there is none. It is by virtue of the common Spirit, the one Spirit that you discover to be present in all of us.

This that you feel among students of The Infinite Way, those from near and those from far—this fellowship, this love that you experience, this joy of companionship in The Infinite Way—is not based on any human values. It is based on their conscious oneness with God, which constitutes their oneness with all other students who meet on the spiritual path, and so you discover that there is no need for a human tie or a human obligation or a human debt.

Because you and your Father are one and all that the Father has is yours, you look within yourself for God's grace. Your relationship with other students is not one of expecting, wanting, or desiring anything of them, but rather, out of the abundance of God's grace, sharing with them that which has been given you. You have the feeling, too, that they are not with you to get anything from you. They come in a free association of love to share the heavenly gifts with you, and so that you may have the opportunity of sharing these with them.

In that relationship there is nothing of a material nature that enters into it as a duty, an obligation, or a necessity. Only in this way can such a bond remain. Because God is unveiled in your consciousness as your identity and as That which supports, sustains, and feeds you, and as you give recognition to the unveiling of God in the consciousness of every student—and realize that he, too, knows the Source of his good and therefore the joy, not of getting, not of seeking, not of acquiring, but of sharing—you begin then, and only then, to perceive what a spiritual relationship can be and will eventually do on earth among men.

Just as this unveiling of the truth of your true relationship with God and with all mankind has taken place in you, some day it will include all of human consciousness. God does not select a personal "you" or a personal "me" for his blessings. God's grace is unveiled that it may be shared by all mankind. True, it comes only into the consciousness prepared for it, but "two or three . . . gathered together in my name" or "ten righteous men" can save a city. So, as consciousness is more and more open to this unveiling of truth, the entire world will be embraced in this same relationship that is now being experienced by students of The Infinite Way.

The Circle of Christhood

In these last few years, wherever Infinite Way teaching was taking place, students have come to me from all parts of the United States and Canada, from all parts of England and Europe, from Africa, Australia, New Zealand, and South America. All drawn by what? By the Spirit of God that had been unveiled in my human consciousness, drawn also by the Spirit of God that was unveiled in the consciousness of those of you who live in each of these countries, drawing all men from all parts of the globe unto you, and then raising them up to the level of your spiritual consciousness, your Christ-consciousness.

As they went home, back to their countries and their cities, these students carried the Grace they had attained in our united consciousness, and they imparted this Grace to the students of The Infinite Way in their cities and their lands, drawing them into this universal brotherhood, fulfilling the circle of Christhood that is revealed in *The Art of Meditation.**

There is such a Circle on the inner plane. There are those with whom we tabernacle who have access to the divine Consciousness of the illumined of all ages. There is a circle of Christhood in which we live and walk and through which we receive revelation and inspiration. It was this that enabled me to write that that Circle would be revealed on earth, and it was given to me to travel this world and form that invisible Circle among Infinite Way students. But it has spread far beyond that group, because the "unveiling" reveals that this Spirit of God is the Spirit of God unto all men. So the circle of Christhood is to embrace all men. Whether or not they ever become students of The Infinite Way, nevertheless they will be drawn into that Circle.

As a link in this circle of Christhood, you will be living in two

*By the author (New York: Harper & Row, 1956), pp. 149–54.

worlds or between two worlds. You will be in this world but not of it. You will be of the spiritual kingdom, and even though you are of the circle of Christhood, you will be living in the world of business, art, literature, government, or religion in order that this light may shine, in order that you may continue to lift up the son of God in all men. You lift It up by beholding the Christ in individual consciousness and as individual consciousness.

It is not that you do any *thing.* You do not have to go out on any good-will missions or save-the-world missions, but wherever you are and whomever you meet, there will be the flicker of an eyelash, a second of recognition, and you will have lifted up the son of God in man. You will have perceived and discerned the Christ incarnate in all the saints and all the sinners you meet, in all the friends and all the enemies you meet. Thus you will not only be more solidly embodied in the circle of Christhood, but you will be drawing into that Circle those who have been outside, the branch of a tree that has been cut off and is withering and dying.

The Purpose of The Infinite Way

Once again let me remind you that the function of The Infinite Way is not merely the healing of disease or the overcoming of sin or of lack. It is a rising out of the three-dimensional consciousness, out of the consciousness of good and of evil, into the Fourth Dimension, the illumined consciousness which is aware of the things of God. In this fourth-dimensional realm, you are in an area of consciousness where you not only know the things of God, but you receive the things of God, and you live under the law of God. This is Grace.

The Master, who of all persons was best known for his realized state of Christ-consciousness, used as his principle "resist not evil" and "put up . . . thy sword," which is a recognition that there is no power out in the world, nothing to fight. He understood the non-power of the world of effect.

You, too, must lay the ax to the root, and the root of all evil is the universal belief in two powers, what Paul called "the carnal mind," the mind of good and evil. Once you understand the principle that all evil is impersonal and that it does not have its rise in any individual, you will begin to have the secret of healing work and the secret of world work, because you will not attach the sin, the disease, the struggle for power, the wrong thinking, or any other thing to an individual.

That which is anti-Christ, or so-called evil, is the carnal mind, the universal belief in two powers, which constitutes a universal hypnotism. When you have thus impersonalized and recognized the nothingness of this universal belief, you have lifted your consciousness closer to the Christ-consciousness, and then you will discover why you do not have to resist evil. God is not in the whirlwind. Power is not in the evil condition. Power, God, is in the "still small voice." Do you want God? Do you want God-power? Do you want God's grace? Then be still! And when the still small voice speaks, you have it. What happens when you are in the inner stillness is that the presence of God is realized, and It does the work, whatever the nature of that work is.

The importance of this principle is far greater than you can imagine. The realization of God is not so that you or anyone else should find health, abundance, or happiness. Be assured that God has no interest in that at all. If, in The Infinite Way, there were ten thousand or a hundred thousand of us who really attained health, wealth, and happiness, it would still not be too great an accomplishment, since there are millions and millions of people on earth and more being born every day. So our individual regeneration would be practically meaningless.

It is only insofar as the light coming to you and to me is permitted to be shown forth in the world that we serve any purpose on earth. We were not sent here just to become happy human beings. We were sent here on earth to glorify God, that God's laws should be made manifest through us and that through us the world might witness the laws of God in operation, the laws that make men free.

There is a mental inertia that operates universally in this human world, preventing even those who have been taught how to prepare themselves spiritually for the day from doing so. This mental inertia makes them forget to realize God's presence; it makes them forget to realize that mesmerism or malpractice is not spiritually ordained, and therefore is not operative in the individual consciousness that has realized the Presence. For the person, however, who does engage in daily spiritual preparation, the realization of the presence of God and the nonpower of mesmerism or malpractice nullifies the effects of universal hypnotism, and in some degree these effects are also nullified for the entire world. A group of diligent students could not only free themselves from discords, but they would gradually free their communities, families, neighbors, friends, nations, and eventually free the world.

Because each of us is so individual, we each play a different part in letting the light of the message shine through us. There are those who may invite members of their family or friends into a group to hear the tape recordings,* and in that way the light goes out into human consciousness. Some are further developed, and they become practitioners and teachers. Still others may aid in the financing of the different activities of the work, and thereby help to send it out around the world. Eventually, there are those who, perhaps with greater discernment than others at the moment, perhaps with greater preparedness, begin to understand the principles of The Infinite Way in such a way that they individually can be instruments in a greater measure to bring divine Consciousness to human experience. Each plays a part, and no one chooses which part he will play. But whatever is given to anyone as his particular forte, that is the manner in which he must function in this message.

*All the lectures and classes of Joel Goldsmith were recorded and are available. —Ed.

Accepting Responsibility for World Work

When this Spirit of God makes Itself evident in us and we come to know that we have a responsibility toward this entire world, we begin to wonder, "How can I fulfill this obligation to the world?" And we may well ask that question, because no one on earth has enough money to provide for and educate all the children of the world. No nation on earth has enough resources to maintain and sustain all the impoverished nations. Therefore we must find a different way of serving, blessing, helping, and raising up the people of the world.

Let us not believe for a moment that by tithing our income, giving away 20 or 50 per cent, or even more, we are doing very much for the world. Even if we had such spiritual healing power as the Master had, and could heal multitudes, we would not be doing too much. We never can reach all the three billions of people in the world either with our money or with our healing gift. There is only one way in which that can be accomplished, and that is through accepting the responsibility of spiritual realization. Everyone at our level of consciousness should be engaging in world work. Whether we do it in a united group or do it individually at home, alone, is not the important thing. The important thing is that it is done.

We are now going through a period that is fascinating and challenging. I would not be surprised if it is not more interesting to be alive at this particular time than at any other time in the history of the world. Certainly this is a period when the world is going through a transition of such proportions that it may be the final transition, that in which material sense is completely overcome and Christ-consciousness comes upon the world as a universal gift.

To me it appears that this is what is happening. For example, there is a great deal of religious upheaval. But with it we can also note the greater sense of unity that is taking place among the religions of the world. How many religious barriers are being removed! Limitations are being broken down in the Catholic Church as never before and, of course, this is being equally matched by a breaking down of the sense of separation in Protestanism. While a good part of the world may call some of these changes heresy and fight them, we know that in reality they are the breaking up of ignorance and superstition.

This is the age of the breaking up of prejudice in race relations. There is a breaking up, too, not only of the type of capitalism that did not adequately care for its workers, but also of the type of unionism that had no consideration for management and employers. It is a breaking up on all sides of the old encrusted patterns of the idea that self-preservation is the first law of human nature.

The human mind and its activities may be likened to a swamp, deep in the forest, a swamp that is cut off from sunshine and fresh air, from even the moon and the stars. It is dark and damp and miserable and abounds in all kinds of inferior creatures. You will recognize these creatures. They are those of whom Paul speaks: "The natural man receiveth not the things of the Spirit of God." This is the human mind, the activities and the creatures of the human mind, but it is made new when Christ has entered in, just as the swamp would be made new and fresh if the blocking trees were cut away and the sun were allowed to shine through.

So, when the mist clears from us and the Christ enters into our soul, our world becomes new. We are no longer a world full of separate persons. We have now become a part of the circle of Christhood, each sharing with the other that which has unfolded within him from the kingdom of God. Since we are a world of individuals, I am receiving the grace of God which I share with you, but those of you who are artists, writers, ministers, business people, or lawyers are receiving the grace of God in different forms, and you share these with one another.

When we understand this, it completes the circle of Christhood. Let us not confine our sharing, however, to those who are already in the Circle, but let us draw into this Circle people of the entire world by our recognition and acknowledgment of the Christ in them. Lifting up the son of God in them draws them into the circle of Light. It may take a week, a month, a year, or ten years before they consciously enter that Circle and acknowledge that they are in and of it, but that is no concern of ours. Once we have lifted up the son of God in them, they have entered our circle of Christhood, and then it is just a matter of time, circumstance, and experience before they will open their eyes and say, "Whereas I was blind, now I see. Whereas I was dead, now I am awake, alive."

We are that swamp until we consciously let the light shine within us and learn to walk with God, talk with God, sleep with God, and awaken with Him, consciously realizing:

Thou art my day; Thou art my night; Thou art the wisdom that guides and governs me. Thou art the Soul that purifies my every thought and deed. Thou art the Spirit that purifies every motive and makes of me a givingness.

When we turn within to the Spirit of God, it is only to receive a grace that we may share, a light and a wisdom. It devolves upon those who have received spiritual light to be transparencies through which that light reaches the world. As it comes to our individual attention that there is some form of so-called evil taking place or about to take place—evil as related to health, to weather, or to human relationships—let us remember that it is a call to us as illumined souls to leave our "nets" immediately and retire into a meditation to bring the activity of the Christ to the situation until that particular problem has been met.

Be Still

There must always be an individual you or me to bring about the realization that in the presence of the realized Christ temporal power is not power. Without the Christ appearing as the consciousness of Jesus Christ, a light would not have come to earth at that particular time in that particular way. Remember that if you have ever called upon a practitioner for physical, mental, moral, or financial help and have received it, it was the realized Christ in the consciousness of that practitioner that did the work. Without the realized Christ in individual consciousness, the human mind would go right on being sick, sinning, and dying.

Only the realized Christ in individual consciousness makes non-power of what has been temporal power. It is for this reason that you cannot separate the Christ from Jesus, you cannot separate the Buddha from Gautama, nor can you separate the Spirit from individual man, for they are one. When you recognize Spirit and man as one, then you have the omnipresence of Omnipotence and Omniscience. You need no words and you need no thoughts: you need the silence of receptivity, the listening ear, and then whatever truth has to be voiced, God voices. But there must be a listening consciousness.

Be still; be still. Do not think thoughts. "Be still, and know that I am God." *I* in the midst of you, *I* am God. Be still. In quietness and in confidence, be still. Stop taking thought, for by taking thought you cannot change anything in the world. You probably will only make it worse than it is. Do not take thought. Be still. Listen for that Voice, and when He utters His voice, the earth melts. This keeps us from becoming egotists and believing that we humanly have power. We are but the instruments or transparencies through which and as which the power can act, and act in proportion to our stillness and our quietness.

Never forget that the Master says, "The Father that dwelleth in me, he doeth the works." This will ever keep you humble. Even if a storm or a war should stop after your meditation, you will know that you did not stop it: you were but the transparency through which the activity of God reached human consciousness.

The Master healed the blind, but he never said, "I healed the blind." He said that it was that the glory of God might be made manifest. Do not forget that—that the glory of God may be made manifest. And how can we be instruments through which the glory of God is made manifest? By being still and knowing:

His Spirit is upon me, and I am ordained to heal the sick, but not without His Spirit being upon me. I am ordained to heal the sick, not by virtue of any words that I know or thoughts that I think, but by virtue of His Spirit being upon me, and then the right words and the right thoughts will come through.

At this stage of unfolding consciousness, you are responsible for every picture that presents itself to your sight or hearing. You may not "pass by on the other side" of the road. It is given to men living purely in the human world to ignore the troubles of their fellow men, especially if they are of a different land, a different religion, or a different race. It is not so given unto you. The Grace which you have received from God was given you, not for you: it was given as the fruitage of God which the world is to eat. "Take, eat; this is my body." You are a fruitful vine on which grapes grow: you are spiritually fed and spiritually clothed and spiritually housed. Give up your grapes; let your grapes go out into the market, into the world.

You owe a debt to God and to the world, and the debt is that you do not pass by on the other side of the road, but take note of every discord and every inharmony and bring to bear the activity of the Christ. Be a transparency through which the Christ dissolves the appearance. You do not necessarily have to think anything, but you must be still. You must be still for an instant, and let His Spirit flow through you and dissolve the appearance. You may not pass by on the other side.

You are at a state of spiritual unfoldment where you have already been told to leave your "nets"—not to go anywhere or do anything, but just not to be concerned about your "nets" in the face of appearances. Rather cease your fishing for a moment and be "fishers of men." And how? Just by recognition. It takes only a moment, the blink of an eye, to realize that in the presence of the Christ, temporal power is not power. It has only the "arm of flesh."

You cannot serve God, whom you have not seen and do not know, except as you serve man, whom you do know. Your only way of serving God is in serving man. This is giving the first fruits unto God. The only way you have of neglecting your service to God is to neglect your service to man.

It is good and right that out of your material resources you share something with those who have less or who have nothing. That is a minor but necessary part of your spiritual development, because we all must acknowledge that we have very little in the way of material resources to give in comparison to the needs of the world.

You who walk in the Light have more to give individually than an entire nation has to give, for the nations can give only of material resources which are limited and finite, but you have living waters, you have spiritual meat, you have spiritual wine, spiritual bread. You have the word of Life; you have the Spirit of God incarnate in you.

Above all, you have a moment of silence, so that in that silence the voice of God may thunder. This is the most precious gift in all the world. You have emptiness. You bring to God every day an empty barrel, an empty consciousness, praying:

Fill me today with all Thou art. Fill me with Thy Soul, with Thy Spirit, with Thy grace that my presence on earth may glorify Thee, that my presence on earth may show forth Thy glory, "with the glory which I had with thee before the world was," the original glory of divine sonship.

You might ask yourself every once in a while, "Why was I born? To what purpose have I come to earth?" If you listen, you will hear the Voice say, "*I* am come that ye might have life, that this world might have life." "Ye" is not just you. "Ye" is all human consciousness. *I* am come that human consciousness may be fulfilled with the Spirit of God, filled full of the Spirit of God. *I* am come that the kingdom of God may come on earth as it is in heaven.

You are not only *on* earth, but you are *of* the earth until the moment comes in which you realize, "the Spirit of God dwells in me." You are the man of earth until the realization has come to you that as man or woman you are nothing—nothing, less than nothing. It is only as the Spirit of God touches your consciousness that you are awakened, enlivened. You are "the walking dead" until the Spirit of God touches you, that through you this Spirit may be allowed to flow to all mankind.

The manner of it is to realize that in the face of every appearance, whenever a human being appears to you, you are to lift up the son of God in him and realize God incarnate in him. Whenever an appearance of sin, disease, death, lack, limitation, or disaster presents itself to you, you are instantly to remember that in the presence of God-realized, in the presence of the realized Christ, temporal power is not power. In heaven or on earth, there is no power greater than *I AM.*

When the Spirit of the Lord God is upon you, you are ordained, but you are not ordained to be set apart. You are ordained to heal the sick, to comfort, to feed, to forgive. That is the purpose of ordination—not that you may be glorified but that you may be better equipped to give more abundantly, to share more freely, to understand more universally that it is not only the children of your flesh who are your children, but that all the children of this world are your children, and you have an equal responsibility to share with them.

You must be able to look out upon this world and say unto it: "The Spirit of God in me is your Father. You may look to the Father within me for substance and sustenance. You, friend or so-called foe, may look to the Spirit of God in me, the fatherhood of God in me, for your care."

Then you will understand this relationship that has been kept secret from the world, the invisible bond that exists among all mystics. The visible and invisible mystics of the world who have recognized *I* standing at the door of their consciousness, are eternally united in consciousness, sharing with one another.

I have set before thee an open door, and no man can shut it.

—Revelation 3:8